RIGHT

from

the

START

**Effective Planning and Assessment
in the Early Years**

RIGHT

from

the

START

Effective Planning and Assessment in the Early Years

Vicky Hutchin

Hodder & Stoughton

A MEMBER OF THE HODDER HEADLINE GROUP

Acknowledgements

The author wishes to give very special thanks to the staff, children and parents at Fortune Park Early Years Centre. She wishes to thank Billy Ridgers for a great deal of moral support, for reading drafts and putting up with with her moans and groans. Thanks are also due to Sindhu Hope and Anne Louka at Ambler Primary School, Perina Holness and children at Marquess Under Fives Education Centre, Caroline Brown at North Islington Nursery School and Angela Lam, Linda Lockie and other early years staff who attended a course on assessment in the early years at the University of London Institute of Education, Autumn Term, 1998.

Orders: please contact Bookpoint Ltd, 130 Milton Park, Abingdon, Oxon OX14 4SB. Telephone: (44) 01235 827720, Fax: (44) 01235 400454. Lines are open from 9.00 – 6.00, Monday to Saturday, with a 24 hour message answering service. You can also order through our website: www.hodderheadline.co.uk

British Library Cataloguing in Publication Data
A catalogue record for this title is available from The British Library

ISBN 0 340 73049 8

First published 1999
Impression number   10   9   8   7   6   5
Year   2005   2004   2003

Copyright © 1999 Vicky Hutchin

Cover photo by Billy Ridgers.
Typeset by Wearset, Boldon, Tyne and Wear.
Printed in Great Britain for Hodder & Stoughton Educational, a division of Hodder Headline, 338 Euston Road, London NW1 3BH, by J.W. Arrowsmith, Bristol.

Contents

Introduction

Oh no, not planning, assessment and record keeping! When will we ever get it right?

Over the past few years the education of three, four and five year olds has become a topical issue. Changes in government policy have resulted in new requirements for those providing education and care for children of this age. This has added to the concern about what is the right thing to be doing for the children. There are particular concerns with regard to planning and assessment – and lots of moans, groans and cries for help from staff grappling with getting this right in the limited time they have available.

There are education inspections on a regular basis for all types of provision which include three and four year olds. There are signs that these are becoming a unifying force among the diversity of services for the children, as all providers are expected to be working towards the same set of objectives for the children's education. In England these objectives are the *Early Learning Goals* which most children should achieve by the end of the Reception year, at the end of the Foundation Stage. Other parts of the UK have their own early years documents.

This book, like the inspection requirements, is designed for everyone working with this age group. Young children of preschool age may attend very different kinds of preschool provision. In some areas there are nursery schools and classes provided by the local authority, in others there are mainly parent-run playgroups and preschools. There is a wide variety of private nursery provision, either in all-day care or in nursery schools, and there are also local authority run day nurseries. Some children stay at home until they start 'big' school. Four year olds can be either with three year olds in nursery or playgroup, or in reception classes alongside five year olds. Each of these settings is likely to be differently organised and managed, and may have staff with different qualifications and training.

The introduction of the Foundation Stage has meant new expectations with regard to curriculum, planning, assessment and record keeping, for every type of early years setting. Good quality observation has been flagged up as an essential part of the assessment process (QCA, 2000). For some, especially in nursery settings, this is an affirmation of what they already do, whilst for others it may be new. The Foundation Stage Profile, the new statutory assessment to be made on every child at the end of the reception year, requires teachers to base their judgements on observations collected throughout the child's time in the Foundation Stage, and particularly in the reception year.

Making the link between assessment and planning is often highlighted as a 'key issue' in inspection reports. Many people feel that the most daunting aspect of their work has been making planning and assessment meet the requirements, whilst still keeping it manageable, 'child-centred', and useful. This book aims to provide the reader with the right support for all the issues raised here. It has practical solutions on how and what to plan and assess in a manageable way, putting the children firmly at the centre of the process. In other words, helping you to 'get it right from the start' for you and for the children, and keeping enjoyment high on the agenda.

How does the book work?

Chapter 1 describes some of the significant developments which have taken place in the early years 'field' recently, especially the new requirements, and what these mean in relation to planning and assssment practice. It also outlines the processes involved in planning and assessment and what 'getting it right' means.

Chapter 2 examines the meaning of 'good practice' in early years settings and how good practice can be achieved. Without a basis in good practice, we cannot have either good planning or good assessment.

Chapter 3 takes a look at one aspect of the planning process: long-term planning. It outlines what needs to be planned at this stage, both in terms of learning and how the 'teaching' will take place.

Chapter 4 takes an overview of the assessment process and record keeping in the early years, and looks at whether different assessment processes may produce different 'results' for the children. It outlines a method for assessment and record keeping which is effective, manageable and does justice to the child's learning, development and achievements. Some examples of what to look for and assess in each area of learning are given.

Chapter 5 looks in more detail at the assessment process outlined in the previous chapter. It shows how to involve parents and children, with examples of real children and real assessments and observations showing the implications for planning 'what next?' for the child concerned. It explains how to set up a manageable record-keeping system.

Having decided on 'what next?' we need to plan for it to happen. **Chapter 6** returns to examine planning – this time the medium- and short-term planning, and how to make these appropriate to the children's stages of development and needs. Once more there are plenty of examples taken from a range of group settings for young children.

Chapter 7 elaborates more fully the link between assessment and planning and outlines a manageable way of doing this. Without this link, what you do may either not support the children's learning or may not be reflected in your written plans as you try to respond better to their needs. And often, if it does not support their learning and build on their interests, they will simply lose interest and find something else to do!

Chapter 8 draws the book to a close, leaving the concluding words to a child.

The following abbreviations and terms are used in this book:

Settings: a 'cover-all' term used to refer to any institutional educational setting for young children, including school reception or nursery class, nursery school, playgroup, day care setting – and anywhere else.

Staff: all those employed to work with children in group settings of any kind.

QCA: Qualifications and Curriculum Authority (formerly the School Curriculum and Assessment Authority).

Ofsted: Office of Standards in Education, responsible for inspections of schools and nursery provision in England and Wales.

DFEE: Department for Education and Employment (England).

LEA: Local Education Authority.

Getting it Right from the Start

1

Getting off to a good start

Whether a child is at a playgroup, day nursery or nursery school or class, whether three, four or five years old, she or he will be at the very beginning of an educational process which will continue for the next thirteen to fifteen years, or more. This places a big responsibility on the shoulders of those who work with children in the 'early years'. How important it is to get the provision we make for these children *right* from the start!

For most children, arriving at nursery, school or playgroup will be their first major experience beyond family and home environment. Getting the planning right for children at this stage means not just having an idea of what you want children to learn and to do, but also knowing about them as people. Each child brings with them a very individual wealth of life experiences, knowledge, understanding and skills. These may be very different from others or they may be quite similar – we will not yet know. So, whatever is planned for the children to do must begin with them as individuals.

The approach each child has to learning – or their 'learning style' – is likely to vary more widely at this age and stage of education than at any other time in the future. This is because children are unlikely to have experienced what it is like to be a member of a group in an 'institutional' setting before. The many shared and common experiences that children will build up through their later educational careers have not yet begun.

Staff in any early years setting need to plan learning experiences for the children in ways which will address differences in learning styles, previous experiences and what motivates them. This means observing the children in action and talking with them and their parents or carers.

Getting education in the early years right

'I enjoyed coming to my nursery. I liked playing with my friends. . ... Best of all I like drawing and pretend in the house and dancing and singing. I like reading books and finding out about minibeasts and . . .'. (Ella, aged 5 years)

Ella dictated this statement to a member of staff in the nursery just before she left to go to primary school. She had been at the nursery since she was three, and this statement was to go into her 'record of achievement', which the nursery would send to her new school. One can tell from her comment that her nursery had been enjoyable and stimulating, as well as an important social experience. It had also helped her to develop a reflectiveness about herself which will undoubtedly be beneficial to her in later school learning and life. All this, and she has only just turned five! Her peers, who were leaving the nursery with her, made similar reflective comments about themselves and their nursery experiences.

There is a great deal of concern at present from practitioners in the early years field about what is right for young children and their early education. It seems obvious, however, that the early years setting about which Ella was talking has in many ways got it 'right', supported by the close links with parents, who also add their comments to the record of achievement.

'I like the birds coming to eat the worms.' (Who would believe this was at an inner-city nursery!) 'Outside there's big bikes to play on and little bikes and scooters. Dance and music and singing with instruments is good too. I like painting on easels too.' (Jack, aged 4 years 8 months)

'I like playing with the train track and I like making a spinner with a battery, crocodile clips and a motor and paper. I like writing abcdefghijklmnopqrstuvwxyz and BMW and making "Who's that tripping-trapping over my bridge?" books.' (Faisal, aged 4 years 10 months)

These statements from four year olds about their preschool experiences have to a large extent depended on carefully thought out provision made by the staff. This was dependent on careful planning which in turn was based on assessments made through observations of the children in action.

Here is an example of how planning and assessment link. In Faisal's record, when he was four years, four months, was the following observation:

'Faisal keeps on returning to science table and display area, trying to make bulbs light up. Sorts through all drawers, exploring the equipment. Knows that buzzer makes sound, so holds it to his ear, but without attaching circuit.'

This was discussed amongst the staff and at the next planning meeting it was decided to continue to focus on making circuits for longer than originally planned, to set up some 'investigations' with the children and make a 'how to make a circuit' book with photos, using Faisal as a 'model'. The book sparked off an interest in a number of other children who had so far not been involved. Almost two terms later his comment above was recorded, showing what an important experience this had been for him. Other observations in Faisal's record showed his interest in writing and how staff helped him to develop his writing skills.

It is planning in this way, tailor made to the needs of individuals but also relevant to many in the group, which is likely to ensure that children are given the kind of preschool experience they need to get them off to a sound start in their future education.

Planning, assessment and record keeping – a chore, or worth the effort?

For staff working in state schools, written curriculum plans are nothing new. Neither is record keeping and assessment. But for those in the private and voluntary sector dealing with under-fives, making written plans and keeping records may well have been introduced only recently.

Most of us who work with young children have chosen to do so because we enjoy it and find it very rewarding. It is the children's excitement and curiosity about the world, their drive to find out about it, and the rapidity of development and change at this age which keeps us going. The planning, assessing and keeping of records – all the written work – can easily represent an unwanted chore which has to be done once the children have gone home.

Yet it doesn't have to be like this! It is this very written work and the discussions between staff in the process of producing it which gives us the necessary time to reflect, develop our thinking and see the differences our work is making to the children. The following comment was made by a member of staff who worked with some of the children quoted earlier:

> *Unless you plan, I don't think you really focus on the children and what they need next in their learning and development. And that means you are unlikely to have appropriate expectations of them or to take their learning forward.*

The staff group also acknowledge that good planning takes time, but is worth every bit of time spent on it.

So planning and assessment can be challenging in a stimulating way, helping you to make what you do relevant and useful to the children, then noting down how they are changing and what they are finding out. It is this which is at the heart of making your work with the children meaningful to both you and them.

What are the expectations and requirements for curriculum planning and assessment of learning?

The new *Early Learning Goals*, replacing the *Desirable Outcomes for Children's Learning on Entering Compulsory School* originally published in 1996, set out the official expectations for children's learning at the end of the Reception year, when most children will have reached the age of five years (QCA, 2000). There are other, similar documents for Wales, Scotland and Northern Ireland.

For England, six *areas of learning* are identified:
- Personal, Social and Emotional Development
- Communication, Language and Literacy
- Mathematics
- Knowledge and Understanding of the World
- Physical Development
- Creative Development

It is up to every institution with three, four and five year olds to devise its own curriculum using the areas of learning listed. The intention is that this will lead the children towards achieving the learning goals by the end of the Reception year. There is an expectation that planning will be organised in this way too, and that assessment and record keeping will chart progress and development in these areas.

Many early years practitioners feel that these 'official' objectives are minimal compared to the array of experiences across a much wider curriculum which they offer to their children. They represent a rather narrow band of (mainly) skills, and only represent a small proportion of what children are learning through the many open-ended experiences usually provided for them. Until recently, many in England were concerned by the absence of reference to *how* children learn or to *play* as an important vehicle for learning. However, the *Curriculum Guidance for the Foundation Stage* (ibid) finally brings England more into line with the Welsh, Scottish and Northern Irish early years documents, where play takes more of a leading position. The areas of learning in each part of the UK are slightly different (see table).

A Comparison of Early Years Curricula

ENGLAND	SCOTLAND
Personal, social and emotional development Communication, language and literacy Mathematics Knowledge and understanding of the world Creative development Physical development	Emotional, personal and social development Communication and language Knowledge and understanding of the world Expressive and aesthetic development Physical development and movement
WALES	NORTHERN IRELAND
Language, literacy and communication skills Personal and social development Mathematical development Knowledge and understanding of the world Physical development Creative development	Personal, social and emotional development Physical development Creative/aesthetic development Language development Early mathematical experiences Early experiences in science and technology Knowledge and appreciation of the environment

Note: the areas of learning are listed in order of priority as published in the original documents.

These documents are subject to change from time to time. Nonetheless, whatever changes occur with regard to requirements, goals or curriculum, these will not affect the need for good planning and good assessment. So, in providing a meaningful and appropriate curriculum for this age group, we must acknowledge that we are providing learning experiences which go *far* beyond the minimum which is required officially. And we must acknowledge the important role that *play* has in young children's learning. Planning, assessment and record keeping *must* reflect this.

What do inspectors look for in terms of planning and assessment?

In England, Ofsted currently organise inspections for all providers of preschool education for children aged four upwards. The inspectors are asked to make judgments on *'the quality and standards'* of the educational provision. They are interested in *'the planning and content of the educational programme. . .'* and their *'judgments should be based on the extent to which the programme is planned effectively . . . in each of the six areas of children's learning for all children.'* They look at *'the extent to which the teaching. . . is planned and organised effectively'* and *'is informed by effective assessments and records of children's attainment and progress.'* They also look at the *'quality of . . . assessment . . .the ways in which children's attainment and progress is assessed'* (Ofsted, 1998).

The chapters which follow are designed to cover all this ground, helping you to plan effectively, and to assess children in the most effective way possible. This book will help you to follow the official advice (SCAA, 1996) that: *'Children's progress and future learning needs are assessed and recorded through frequent observation and are shared regularly with parents'* and *'Children are encouraged to think and talk about their learning. . . .'*

The challenges of planning and assessment for early years practitioners

Since the official requirements were first published, I have run many inservice training courses for staff from schools, daycare and education services, playgroups and community run nurseries on how to address them. Most frequently of all, I have been asked to give advice and support on planning, assessment and record keeping for under-fives. It is these issues which, across the variety of provision, have caused the greatest concern and anxieties.

Very little advice from official bodies (such as QCA and DFEE) has been forthcoming, until very recently, on how to meet the requirements. Many practitioners have told me how they find the 'written work' a struggle. This is not confined to staff in nurseries and playgroups, with less experience of planning and record keeping, but is also often found in schools.

Making the link between written assessments and planning is seen as particularly difficult, although many practitioners are very good at doing this in an informal, immediate and unwritten way. Some experienced early years staff feel that written plans created long in advance make it difficult to respond to children's specific needs as they should. On the other hand, some find building on children's interests (as officially recommended) difficult, as they can seem so diverse.

But more than anything, the difficulty for most people seems to lie in being able to plan for *prescribed* outcomes or goals, as well as linking planning to the assessments and record keeping you have made on the children you work with. This difficulty, however, is nothing new. It is a difficulty which besets teachers of children in all age groups.

The way in which assessments and record keeping in schools have traditionally been kept has not helped. Often records are in folders or files shut away in the cupboard or filing cabinet, from which it is difficult to access specific information easily and quickly. Sometimes beautiful, carefully written records have been kept with attractively mounted samples of the children's work, but these are only used when writing an end of year summary for parents and the next class or school. This means that planning and teaching are much more likely to depend on what staff have *felt* is appropriate and to rely on memory of what the children have been doing, rather than based on actual written evidence. It can all be a bit hit or miss, as the staff have to trust their memories of what every child does in a busy setting.

What is needed instead is a systematic link between record keeping and planning, which is easy for all staff to manage – something which the following chapters will outline.

From planning to assessment and back again

The quality of education depends upon the way in which assessment of children as learners informs the curriculum.

(Lally and Hurst, 1992)

Assessment is the key to whether the curriculum has any relevance at all to the children for whom it exists. Planning the curriculum is at its most effective when it is based on what we know about the development, learning and personality of the children in our care. In fact, it is when planning is fine-tuned to the children that it really becomes rewarding and interesting, and thus enjoyable. If planning was only a question of taking some predetermined learning intentions, and then presenting some predetermined activities for the children to carry out, it would be dull drudgery indeed!

Planning helps me to organise my thoughts and helps me to pick up on what the children like doing and take this forward. Sometimes, though, we might plan to do one thing in a particular way, but it goes in another direction.   (A nursery teacher)

When planning and record keeping work well, staff will have noted the direction things did go in and decide at their next meeting how to follow this up. The new direction could lead to meeting the same learning intention in a different way or to a different learning intention. Good early years planning means that any learning intention can be returned to at another time.

The Rumbold Report (1990) pointed out how young children do not just respond to what we plan to teach:

Children are affected by the contexts in which learning takes place, the people involved in it, and the values and beliefs which are embedded in it. . . . The process of education – how children are encouraged to learn – is as important as, and inseparable from the content – what they learn.

From assessment to planning and back again means that staff are aware of how children have been 'affected' by the learning opportunities they have been offered.

What do we need to plan?

Planning for any age group is usually seen as taking place for three different time scales – long-term, medium-term and short-term – all of which link together. Part of the planning is deciding how the learning environment – the areas of provision inside and in the outdoor area – are to be organised, as well as how the staff will be involved in presenting the learning. This is how you will meet all the learning intentions, and how children will be able to choose what to do to initiate their own learning.

Long-term planning is perhaps best seen as the learning intentions and possibilities to which all children are entitled, often over a year, or over the whole time the child will be in the setting.

Medium-term planning is more practical, in that it is how the long-term overview of learning is turned into practical learning intentions over a shorter period of time – sometimes a term, a half term or even a month. It means identifying and building on children's interests and needs, as well as offering what you want them to learn and find out about.

Short-term planning is much more immediate and responsive to the individual children within the setting, because this is weekly and daily planning, fine tuned to the immediate needs of children and what has been happening from day to day.

All these forms of planning require time set aside from working with the children and some writing. There is one more level or stage of planning which takes place and that is **immediate planning**. This is rarely thought of as planning as it is not written down, but it is what you do and say as you are working with the children. When your medium- and short-term plans are based on information gathered about the children's learning and your reflections on what it might be appropriate to offer them next, they can be used to inform the way you interact with the children from moment to moment. This is the outcome of all the hard work, the discussion and the writing. It is this which can make all the difference to furthering a child's experience and development.

What do we need to assess?

All children deserve to be assessed on everything that they do in the setting – in their self-chosen activities which staff have set up for them to select from, inside and outside, as well as in the staff-led activities presented.

One of the major differences between early years provision, both in and out of school settings, and later schooling is that the staff put thought and energy into setting up certain areas of provision – such as a home corner, block area, sand and water – for children to access for themselves at will. Looking at recent guidelines on teacher assessment for teachers working with 8–11 year olds, what is recommended is to assess the children against the learning objectives to be taught *directly* by the teacher. In the early years, this is only part of your assessment practice. If in play, as Vygotsky (1978) stated, children operate *'beyond their years'* or at their highest level, then it is very important to observe and assess children in their play as well as in all other activities.

Assessment needs to be based on observations of the children in the full range of activities, provision and experiences available. The DFEE, QCA, Ofsted and other official bodies all recommend that assessment is based on active observation. The many different ways of doing this, and making it manageable, are outlined in Chapter 4.

Linking assessment to planning

If planning the curriculum and assessing the children's learning are to be really effective, they must be firmly rooted in what is considered as *good early years practice*. Planning, implementing the plans and assessing the children are all part of one whole process that must fit together smoothly. What the children can learn is dependent on *what* is provided and *how* it is provided – on the planning and the practice. The way we assess and what we can assess is dependent on our planning and practice too. These points can be illustrated in a circular diagram or wheel to show how each part relates to the next (Figure 1.1). There is nothing new in any of this – all that has been done is to make explicit what is often taken for granted, but not necessarily acted upon.

To demonstrate how each element in this cycle link together, here is an example:

PRACTICE
- Implementing the plans
- The learning environment inside and outside
- Play provision
- Resourcing activities and learning experiences
- Child-initiated experiences and activities
- Adult-initiated experiences and activities

PLANNING
- Learning intentions/objectives
- The adult's role in supporting learning
  resulting in a mix of
  – child-initiated experiences and
    activities
  – adult-initiated experiences and
    activities inside and outside

ASSESSMENT
- Observations
- Quick notes on achievements
- Conversations and dialogue
- Children's self-evaluations
- Samples of work
- Deciding 'what next?'

EVALUATING THE PLANS
- Evaluating written plans – medium- and short-term:
  did they help children to learn?
- Evaluating what was learnt in self-chosen activities
  in adult-initiated activities
- Deciding 'what next?'

Fig 1.1   *The planning-practice-assessment cycle*

*Joining in with friends involved in making hats and masks, **Joseph** became involved in an activity which required some cutting. He gave the scissors to a member of staff, saying 'cut it for me, please.' When the staff member asked him to make a start and then she would help, his actions showed that he was not confident in holding the scissors or in cutting effectively.*

This observation was discussed at the next planning meeting, and the staff also recalled how interested Joseph had become in playing board games with dice, which had been part of a recent maths focus on counting. He frequently asked staff and other children if they would play a game with him. It was decided that a learning intention for Joseph for the following week would be developing skills and confidence in cutting. Bearing in mind his interest in board games, it was decided that Joseph should be involved in making a board game with some other children, which would require him to practise cutting. One of the staff-directed activities the following week was to get Joseph to help make a new dice game using gummed paper which needed cutting into rectangles, triangles, squares and circles. The staff decided which other children who needed similar help with cutting should join in.

Through this discussion, all staff were made aware that Joseph needed to be helped to gain confidence and skill in using scissors. Support and encouragement in this was likely to be needed from staff over several weeks in many different situations.

The following comment was recorded a month later in Joseph's record:

Used scissors very well unaided when cutting round a drawing.

Providing for Learning

2

We often talk in relation to early years education about *good practice* and even *best practice*, but what is meant by *practice* and what makes it *good* or *best*? Let us begin by looking at some definitions. *Curriculum* and the idea of *practice* are often thought of as closely linked. *Curriculum* is usually taken to mean what we want children to learn, and *practice* to mean how we put that curriculum into effect. However, they are not always explained in these ways.

Defining 'practice' and 'curriculum'

For children over statutory school age, the National Curriculum in England and Wales specifies what children are to be taught in different subjects at each stage of their education. This then leads, supposedly, to specified outcomes expressed in terms of 'level descriptions' against which children are assessed at certain points during the education process (at the end of Key Stage 1, 2, 3 or 4). It is assumed that it is the teaching of the curriculum which is likely to result in these outcomes for children's learning, so long as the teaching is 'good'!

In a leaflet for early years providers, *An Introduction to Curriculum Planning*, the Qualifications and Curriculum Authority (1998) define curriculum as:

> *A curriculum is the experiences, opportunities and activities that you offer in your educational programme to help children learn and develop.*

However, for providers of preschool education there is no prescribed curriculum as there is for older children. Instead, there is just a set of outcomes or goals which children and staff are to work towards.

So, what does *'experiences, opportunities and activities'* really mean?

The National Children's Bureau (1989) defined curriculum in a way which emphasises that children learn from everything we and they do – from the whole of our practice:

    ‘ *The curriculum for young children includes:*
- *all the opportunities for learning and development that are made available to children;*
- *the activities, attitudes and behaviour that are planned, encouraged, tolerated, ignored or forbidden;*
- *the way the room is organised and the routines followed by children and adults;*
- *the part adults take in organising, directing, influencing and joining in what the children do;*
- *the extent to which parents are involved in each of the above.*

It is from this, however planned or unplanned, consistent or inconsistent, that children learn. ’   (National Children's Bureau, 1989)

This definition is particularly useful as it points out how children learn from everything, whether or not the adults intend this! Using this definition, the boundary between curriculum and practice becomes blurred and we focus more on what children are likely to gain from being in the setting. It clarifies the importance of relationships (between adults and children and between the children themselves), as well as our 'ethos', management style and rules and how we implement these. It helps us to concentrate in more depth on children's learning, rather than looking only at the content of what we plan. It also helps to make us aware that *practice* is a dynamic process which needs to change and develop in the light of our own and the children's evaluations of it: what they did or did not learn, find out or show interest in.

This broader view of curriculum intertwined with practice is also supported by advice given in the Rumbold Report (1990):

    ‘ *The educator must pay careful attention not just to the content of the child's learning, but also to the way in which that learning is offered to and experienced by the child.* ’

Starting from how children learn

During the first six years of life, growth and development takes place in humans at a rate and by an amount which is faster and more significant than at any other stage of life. This refers to all aspects of development – physical, emotional, social, linguistic as well as intellectual. When we talk about children of three and four we are talking about children who are right in the middle of this phase – and who will continue to grow and develop throughout the period of their early education. For practice to be 'good', it has to start from *how* children learn.

What we know from research

Research has long established that young children learn best under certain conditions. These include being given opportunities to explore and experiment for themselves and be actively involved in first-hand experiences. They need to be able to make sense of their experiences if they are to learn. Adults can help by ensuring the learning context is meaningful, familiar and relevant.

Learning for young children needs to be presented holistically, not as separate subjects, because this is the way in which children learn. Donaldson (1978) and Wells (1986) have shown us how children can operate at much higher levels of understanding and with greater skill if what we are trying to show and teach them is *meaningful* to them. Here is an example of a child involved in carrying out a chosen task which is relevant and meaningful to her.

Sally *(4 years 2 months)*

Sally is at the creative workshop where children can help themselves to a range of materials with which to create whatever they wish. An adult is nearby. As she works, completely engrossed in what she is making she talks to the adults and other children about the materials, and what else is going on around her. She uses a range of tools, including a hole puncher, scissors, stapler and felt tips, tape and glue as she creates a present for her mother's birthday. 'I'm making something' she says. She uses plastic cartons, straws, paper and card. Halfway through she discovers she can join two straws by poking the ends into each other.

'Look, I've made a square. . .no, I know it's a bracelet – it's for you' and she hands it to the staff member. When she has finished her present

she says: 'I cut the big straws because they were too long. They could poke in someone's eyes.'

As Sally works at her self-initiated 'project' you can see how the curriculum for her is interwoven. In her handling of tools she is using physical skills with dexterity. Her linguistic skills are used to explain, describe, reason, surmise, imagine and ask questions of others about what they are doing. Her social skills are demonstrated by her use of talk to others to involve them in conversation, and interest them in what she is doing as well as to inquire about them. She demonstrates practically some mathematical skills – comparing lengths, for example, and using mathematical language. She uses many of the skills required in *Knowledge and Understanding of the World* to do with designing and making. All this is in a creative activity. This observation demonstrates how the learning process *requires* an integrated curriculum in order to be really successful. All children *learn* through social interaction with adults and their peers, through talk and through play.

Meeting developmental needs

Children of three, four and five have developmental needs which must be met. There are aspects of their development – especially those to do with maturity and physical development – which in no way reflect on a child's ability or intellectual capacity. For example, with regard to **physical development**, by the age of three most children can walk well and run, and are developing their balancing skills, but skills in hopping, skipping, throwing and catching will probably be at an early stage. This is just one example of the kind of developmental need that will have to be planned and provided for.

In their **language development** most children will have learnt to talk competently in sentences by the age of three. Some children will have already learnt to communicate to a fluent level in more than one language, and others will be learning English as an additional language as they begin school or nursery. However, for all children much still remains to be learnt in terms of more complex grammatical structures and vocabulary, as well as how to use a variety of ways in speaking to a range of audiences.

Emotionally, from their earliest moments young children have usually developed close relationships with a limited number of people, most commonly their parents, close family members and carers. Meeting emotional needs means taking seriously the issue of settling children into a new setting and helping them to separate from parents and carers. This needs to be seen as an integral part of the educational provision.

How adults support young children to learn and develop

Gordon Wells (1986) compares the way adults support young children in their language development to playing ball with them. The adult has to run to catch the ball when the child throws, but has to throw direct into the child's arms for the play to be successful. This illustration shows us the kind of 'scaffolding' adults need to give children in *all* their learning. It needs to be at just the right level: not doing things for the children, or leaving them floundering and unable to achieve, but supporting them just enough.

Sometimes this could mean the adult giving a running commentary, talking through a process with a child as it is happening (*'First we do. . . then we . . .'*) in order to model the words for the child. At other times, letting the child take the lead in informing adults about their own areas of expertise can be a tremendous support for their social and personal development and self-confidence. I can think of many occasions when three year olds have taught me words in their own first languages, or the names of dinosaurs and how to identify them, or recounted the story of a cartoon film I didn't know.

Creating a stimulating learning environment

In an early years setting, the learning environment is always considered as an essential ingredient in provision for learning, with many activities, facilities and areas of the room and outside set up so that children can choose to play with or without adults.

Recently I produced a handout for a course on the early years learning environment in which I made a list of all the forms of provision a well-resourced nursery setting was likely to offer at any one time. The list numbered 25 different activities and areas of provision, inside and outside.

However, it is the display and presentation of materials and resources for learning (what Pat Gura calls *'stuff'*) and what we allow the children to do with the 'stuff' which is as important as the 'stuff' itself. Gura (1996) points out that we could compile a list of characteristics for the right kind of materials for young children's learning, but *'the materials do not work **for** us, we each have to learn to work **with** them, in what we believe is the best interests of the children.'*

So, providing a stimulating environment means not just making the provision available, but showing we value it. The amount of status given to, for example, the sand play, is perhaps most easily noted by the amount of time staff spend there. And the ways in which the staff and other adults involve themselves in play or with an activity can make the difference between a stimulating and unstimulating environment.

This is, of course, only part of the story of creating a rich learning environment. A stimulating environment enables children to celebrate and share their experiences of their own cultures, languages and heritages. It also reflects and celebrates the cultures and languages in the local community and the multi-ethnic nature of British society.

In order to try and ascertain the foundations of *good practice* we have looked very briefly at some aspects of child development, at how adults can support children's learning and at the need for an exciting and relevant learning environment to be established. Now we turn to what research tells us about how to make practice *good*.

Getting practice right from the start

Research defines 'good practice'

Kathy Sylva notes from her own research how good quality preschool provision can promote motivation and perseverance, knowing how to learn, social skills and positive attitudes to self. She has shown how this has a lasting and deep-rooted effect on children's future education and beyond (Jowett and Sylva, 1986). Good practice then must foster these skills and attitudes to learning.

Gillian Pugh (1997), summarising a wide range of research on young children's learning, noted the following points as forming a bedrock for good practice:

- placing an emphasis on **personal, social and emotional** development;
- **starting from the child,** taking what he or she *'already knows, understands and can do'* and *'individual children's thoughts, feelings, learning, development, and achievements'* as the basis for planning;
- providing *'opportunities for children to make **responsible choices** from among a wide range of activities';*
- recognising *'the **importance of play** in children's learning, and in the development of the capacity to imagine, explore and experiment, to make loving and co-operative relationships, to understand and express a variety of feelings and ideas';*
- **ensuring equality** in access to learning for all children, as they *'develop in different ways, reflecting their own families, communities and cultures, and at their own pace'.*

All these aspects of child development and learning need to be addressed if practice is to be effective in helping children develop to fulfil their potential and to acquire an attitude of enthusiasm about their own learning. The next section illustrates some of these points with examples of children learning in a variety of settings – all of which are striving to make their practice 'good' (and are succeeding!).

Prioritising personal, social and emotional development

Figure 2.1 shows Billie engaged in role play with another child at nursery. Their game involved dressing up, and here she is helping her playmate using her own newly acquired physical skills in order to keep the play going. They are both gaining practice in sustaining social interaction and in how to keep play going by accepting or giving help to each other.

Starting from the child

Learning opportunities must build on children's past experiences – what they already know, can do and understand – if they are to be useful. They must also build on what motivates each child as an individual. This means finding out about children from their

Fig 2.1
Developing social skills

parents and carers. It means staff making time to observe and listen, as part of the daily routine. Julie Fisher (1998) states that this is one of the primary roles of the teacher in 'teaching' the children. Observing children, talking to their parents and the children themselves is vital, and the information gathered must be used to inform the short- and medium-term planning.

Children are motivated to learn about what interests them most. Sometimes this may be most obvious in a child's particular choice of activity or play over a period of time. Here are some examples:

Joseph's *main interest was board games which he wanted adults and others to play with him; he also wanted to make up his own (see Chapter 1).*

For **Billie** *(see Figure 2.1) role play was a motivating force (which usually involved homes, families and shopping trips).*

*For **James**, it was role play of a different nature which motivated him, taking super heroes and cartoons as his starting point (Hutchin, 1996).*

***Faisal's** interests were obvious not so much in what he chose to do but in the way he approached everything (Hutchin, 1996). His motivation to learn seemed to be in looking for certain patterns everywhere. At one point it was patterns with straight lines (often grids), at another time it was matching pairs of things which he would look for or create.*

Faisal's approach to what he did, showed the underlying *'schemas'* by which he was organising his thoughts. Schemas refer to the *'basic mental framework'* which structures early learning (Gura, 1996) or *'threads of action and thought'* (Nutbrown, 1994). As Gura puts it: *'Learning develops as a result of attempting to match patterns from the world outside to the schemas in our heads.'*

Fig 2.2
Faisal's drawing

Some children, like Faisal, follow their schematic concerns through everything they do in a much more obvious way than others. Faisal's search for patterns, making connections between new things in which he had identified a pattern with other things he already knew was obvious to all who worked with him. He also found a way to express this to others in both English – which was new to him – and Bengali. For a period of time his interest was in parallel lines and grids as well as pairs of things. This could be seen in his drawing, painting, collage and 3D modelling, building with blocks, using construction sets, imaginative small world play with a dolls house, cars and trains, physical play and even organising the milk cartons on the drinks table! We need to know about and record these interests and schemas, whatever form they take, for the children we work with.

We must also find out what they *can* already do. We must then use this information in our planning if we want to make a difference to the children's learning.

Aileen *(3 years 10 months)*

On an outing with a member of staff and small group of children, Aileen showed interest and excitement in everything she passed. She chatted to the other children and adults in a more relaxed manner than at school. Her use of positional language was particularly noticeable throughout the journey, for example going over the footbridge and through the tunnel under the railway:

'We're on top of the cars now.' 'We're under the trains.' *Also counted steps on the footbridge – up to 12.*

Once the staff were aware of her skills and the interest the outing had generated in her, they were able to plan a number of learning opportunities and events to involve her and other children. These included making books about journeys, using lots of positional language. The teacher recreated the story of the outing at story time, using small world play figures to represent the staff member and children. She involved Aileen in more advanced counting activities than were presented to her before. Aileen's confidence in the class grew enormously as a result.

Making responsible choices

The following observation, made when Lucy was three years, eight months, shows how children do make responsible choices if we allow them to. The nursery which she went to made outdoor and indoor provision available to the children all day.

Lucy loved outdoor play and rarely chose to play inside whatever the weather. There was always some form of writing and drawing materials provided outside as well as books either on a blanket with cushions in a comfortable corner or on a table with chairs. Her mother worried about her missing out on 'table' activities inside and that this would hold up her development in literacy in particular. However, it did not take long before she became involved in not only looking at the books provided and asking for one to be read to her, but also drawing with chalk on the ground, then writing letters from her name on message pads in role play. Once, for example, she used 'strings of Os and Ls' and told a member of staff that it was a story about Rosie and Jim.

The importance of play

Role play was all-important to this group of children. Here Billie is with a group of friends in the home corner.

Billie is wrapping up a 'baby' (doll). Danielle explains the play to a staff member: 'Samantha's the mummy and we're the kids.'
Billie: 'And the mummy's had a baby.'
Samantha to Billie: 'Wrap that baby up.'
She does so and Danielle goes off whilst the others go to bed.
Staff member asks 'Where has Danielle gone?'
Samantha: 'She's gone to London Bridge. . .'.
Billie: 'She's gone across London Bridge and I'm having hot chocolate.'
Samantha shouts to Danielle 'Come home when you've finished at London Bridge, won't you!'.

The member of staff who made this observation noted how the play had been developing throughout the morning (for well over an hour) and how satisfying it had been for all participants, as it flowed on to different topics and back again. These children were sharing their own individual knowledge about nursery rhymes (or could it be places?), about life in general and relationships, talking and acting together. At points the play involved writing and drawing, dealing with shape, number and quantity, visits outside, dressing up and putting on bandages for 'bad arms'. And all this was only what the staff member had managed to observe in a busy setting.

Access to learning for all children

Children need to be able to access all the learning opportunities which are offered. All children require support to learn, but different kinds of support and different amounts of support will be needed for different children. For any one child, more support will be needed in some areas of development and learning than others. An important aspect of helping children to access what is available is to make it meaningful by ensuring their home experiences are valued, celebrated and reflected in the learning environment.

Mohammed and his family had recently arrived in the country. He was finding the whole process of a new place to live and coming to nursery a little scary, especially as no child or adult in his nursery, where there were many bilingual children, shared the same language as him and his family (Tigrinya). In order to help him settle, the nursery borrowed favourite tapes of music from his parents, and his parents brought in photos of his family for him to keep at the nursery. The nursery made a photo book about him in the nursery for him to take home. Later on, with help from a local community organisation, his mother translated some of the children's favourite storybooks into the family's home language and helped the nursery extend its collection of bilingual story tapes by recording one or two stories for them. All this helped Mohammed gain access to the learning experiences on offer, and helped to build up the resources of the nursery for all.

The staff in this nursery regularly evaluated their provision to ensure that all children had equal access to the learning opportunities. They did this by monitoring the use of provision inside and out, checking *how* boys and girls used it, making sure less confident children were able to use all provision, and ensuring bilingual children were supported as necessary to join in group play and activities. They also checked, with the help of parents, that the cultures of the children and of the wider community were reflected in the resources and regularly reviewed.

The observations just described show how the principles of good practice, backed up by research findings on children's learning, operate in action. None of the learning experiences and events described would have been successful unless they met children's developmental needs. These were provided in a stimulating learning environment where children have access to a mix of adult-led and self-chosen, self-initiated play and activities, carefully planned. Planning and assessment must support this good practice, to be effective, and this is what we will look at next.

What is effective planning?

In order for the examples of learning considered above to have taken place, planning was required. This was *effective* planning: it built on children's interests, inquisitiveness, delights as well as their existing skills and knowledge. Planning which is 'right' means it is planning which works! It takes on board the full range of skills, attitudes, understanding we know is appropriate for children of this age. It includes the learning that is to be 'presented' to the children and what staff will do to ensure it happens in practice. Let us look at some of the principles on which planning must be based in order to be effective.

Planning is most effective when:

■ *'The child is at the centre of curriculum planning rather than the child has to fit in with school demands'* (Lally and Hurst, 1992). This is equally important in all stages of planning – long-medium- and short-term.
■ It is based on an understanding of how children learn and develop at this age.
■ The medium- and short-term plans build on what we know about the children we are working with, their interests, existing knowledge and skills and their needs – emotional, physical, social as well as learning needs. In other words, it means using our records and assessments to help us plan.
■ It is shared between all those who work with the particular group of children for whom it applies. (Although it may be difficult to involve *everyone* on a regular basis, this should still be the aim, so that all can contribute and develop a common understanding of what has been planned. Everyone will have different strengths, ideas and perspectives to bring to it.)
■ It involves regular evaluation, resulting in adjustments to the medium- and short-term plans to meet the children's needs and interests while keeping the long-term plans as the learning to which all are entitled.
■ It covers different areas of provision, not just table activities. It includes the involvement of staff in play situations such as small world play, water and sand, outdoor play and role play.

- The learning intentions for children are made clear to all but remain flexible enough to meet the needs of every child.
- It involves and informs parents, children and all staff.
- It involves all aspects of learning and doesn't just concentrate on the measurable skills highlighted in the Early Learning Goals. This means it values the *process* of learning, not just outcomes, and involves planning for developments in attitudes to self and to learning.

Successful practice doesn't just rely on good planning, but needs to have effective assessment and record-keeping processes. So what are the principles which underpin good assessment?

What is effective assessment?

Assessment is at its most effective when:

- It is based on what is seen or heard and thus records what the child *can* do rather than what they *cannot* do. Therefore every statement is positive and shows both achievements and where support is needed.
- Parents' contributions to the records and their knowledge of their child is central not only at the beginning, when the child is first admitted, but throughout the child's early educational experience.
- The child is involved, informed about what is written and given a space to express their own view on their achievements.
- The parents and child, and not a predetermined list of skills against which a child is ticked off, form the starting point.
- Staff observe children as part of their daily routine, keeping notes and samples on all aspects of development as they happen: in play, in self-initiated and self-chosen activities and adult-directed activities
- It is based on observations of the child in action. There should be no pressure to set up assessment tasks to see if the child can perform in testing situations, nor to fill in particular charts and tick lists at particular times.
- Notes on significant developments are taken as they happen.
- It is shared regularly with both child and parents.
- It is used for planning the learning experiences which will be offered to the children.
- A manageable system is devised for record keeping and assessment based on the above principles.

■ The preschool records are used to feed the Baseline Assessment which has to be carried out in the reception class.

Here is an example of the cycle in action:

Kieran's interest in minibeasts had been noticed during the Easter holidays by his parents and it was obvious from the first day of term that this was continuing! At a planning meeting the staff decided that this was an important interest to follow up which many children were motivated by. Many investigations and minibeasts hunts followed, setting up a vivarium and a wormery, providing reference books and outings too. And Kieran was used as an expert by other children. 'I found a worm!' 'Take it to Kieran' was often heard. A whole variety of individual and group made books developed as a result. This was supported by using story books such as The Very Hungry Caterpillar, by Eric Carle (1974), and many children made up their own stories.

Looking back over a classful of records on individual children, one could see how many children became involved and how much knowledge and understanding as well as skills in observing, describing, hypothesising and investigating had been developed in so many children. However, this was only part of what was going on – other children's interests and all the children's learning needs were also followed up.

Knowing about child development

An understanding of child development from 0 to 6 years is very important for all staff working with young children. The next chapter looks at long-term planning – the planning which gives an overview of expected and appropriate learning, for which knowing about child development in theory and practice is essential.

Planning the Overview

3

> *Long-term planning is concerned with children's entitlement to a broad and balanced curriculum* (Fisher, 1998).

It is essential to have long-term planning if short-term and medium-term planning are to be effective.

Although there are many aspects to long-term planning, such as early years curriculum policies, action plans from inspections and school or nursery development plans, this chapter concentrates on the long-term overview of appropriate learning and how to go about writing it. Margaret Edgington (1998) gives a comprehensive outline of the broad spectrum of long-term planning. All of these are equally important, but, as there is much to do and it all requires time, certain aspects of this planning need to be prioritised. The priority for all kinds of early years settings, I believe, is developing the overall *learning intentions* for all areas of learning. This will help all staff involved to see the breadth of learning possibilities in each area and what the aims are for all the children.

In a nursery or playgroup setting, the time scale for long-term planning usually means the whole of the children's time with you (probably a year or more). In a primary school setting this should cover the complete Foundation Stage – i.e. the two-year span of nursery and reception classes. This is the pre-National Curriculum stage of education.

What is long-term planning?

Long-term planning is significantly different in nature from medium- and short-term planning – this is why a whole chapter is devoted to it. Some of the differences are:

- It is more generalised. As all children have an entitlement to it, it is not linked to the specific needs of the children in the group but generalises what all children have a right to learn.

- It sets out clearly *what* it is intended that children should learn and only in general terms focuses on *how* it will be done. The *detail* of exactly how and when it will be done, goes into the short-term planning.
- It is closely linked to our understanding of child development.

Why have long-term planning?

In my recent experience of working with staff from many different settings, concerns are often expressed in relation to short- and medium-term planning (especially how to keep it manageable and meet inspection requirements), but there has been much less concern relating to devising long-term plans. This is because it is not always done! There is often a feeling that long-term plans have already been defined adequately by the QCA's *Curriculum Guidance for the Foundation Stage* or the sets of guidelines which many LEAs and some early years organisations have produced. Although these are all undoubtedly useful documents to draw upon and use as guides, it is *not* the same as devising your *own* planning, which is pertinent to *your* setting, with all staff involved in working it out together. This process usually leads to vital discussions on learning, often helping to develop everyone's understanding and to decide on the priorities for learning. It also means pooling ideas on how best to put the plans into action.

Sometimes, in primary schools, long-term early years planning has been seen as part of the whole-school planning for the National Curriculum. Although this may be intended to show progression across the school, there is a tendency for it to be inappropriately driven by the requirements for older children rather than seeing early learning as a phase of learning in its own right. The broader curriculum areas used in the early years such as the six areas of learning used in the Desirable Outcomes and Early Learning Goals, unlike the National Curriculum, highlight the importance of personal, social and emotional development and language (as opposed to English) development.

Early years practitioners sometimes say that long-term planning will result in prescribing inappropriately what children should be doing at certain points in time, regardless of their previous experience or interests, thus removing any flexibility. Some of the reasons given below on the importance of long-term planning help to show how it can be used to *support*, rather than hinder, flexibility. However, there is one simple point to make first: everyday work for the staff in any setting will be made easier if long-term planning is given priority. Without it, the medium and short-term planning will be very demanding tasks.

Focusing on the *learning* you wish children to experience over the whole period of time they are with you is the main purpose of long-term planning.

What you intend children to learn can be presented in a myriad of ways, provided that the long-term planning does not specify *how* it has to be taught or when. There is sometimes a tendency to plan activities or topics rather than the actual learning intentions – thus planning how something will be taught, rather than the learning itself. This is not the point of long-term planning. The learning intentions should show progression, but there is no need to specify in advance exactly when certain learning should take place. The children will be at such different stages in their learning that it would be unhelpful to do so and lead to unnecessary inflexibility. Knowing that the learning has to be planned for at some point during any child's time with you is enough at this stage of advanced planning. The when and how come into the short-term planning.

■ Specifying learning intentions draws the attention of all staff, parents and managers to what the staff and the school, nursery or playgroup is there for – the children's long-term learning.
■ It will help staff to see their role in helping children to achieve. It will show them the breadth of learning possibilities which they should be supporting as they work with the children.
■ It will give staff an idea of *why* they are doing what they do, thus helping them to develop what they do from a basis of understanding, rather than something which has been imposed.
■ It will help staff to coordinate their team work.
■ It will help staff talk to the children about their current learning, development and achievements. It will also help them when they talk to the parents about the children's learning.
■ It will help others who are not so involved see the purpose of early years education and what the staff actually do in early years settings.

To summarise, the emphasis for long-term planning must be on the learning itself, through agreeing and writing up learning intentions rather than focusing on how or when the learning will take place. This is why a knowledge of child development is so important.

What to include in long-term planning

Long-term planning needs to include every area of learning and to ensure there is breadth within each of these. The first job will entail listing, for each curriculum area, the learning intentions you wish children to have experience over, for example, a year. Alongside this there should be a brief outline of how it will take place – not by suggesting topics and activities, but by outlining in general terms how the learning environment and the experiences will be organised, as well as the types of strategies staff will use to support the children's learning.

Curriculum areas

The aim is to give an overview of all appropriate learning, using the six *areas of learning*. Although the point has already been made strongly in Chapter 2 that children's learning is not compartmentalised into areas of learning or subjects, long-term planning is about what adults intend the children to learn. The areas of learning will not be *taught* as discrete subjects, but it is useful to write in this way to clarify for ourselves that we have planned for a full breadth of curriculum.

Aspects of learning

Learning can be seen as composed of various aspects. Most commonly these are seen as knowledge and understanding, skills and attitudes. Dividing each curriculum area into these aspects will help to ensure that they are catered for adequately. If this is not done, one aspect – for example skills – may easily be over-emphasised at the expense of creating the broader view of what it means to learn.

In learning something, all these aspects may have come into play together, but it is equally possible that only one or two aspects are significant. It is not that each aspect will be taught separately, but highlighting these aspects will help to clarify to all – staff, parents and others – the factors which make up learning.

Amina *(3 years 8 months)*

Amina said she couldn't draw herself (often does emergent writing but very rarely draws). Then drew this picture, talking to the staff member

Fig 3.1
Amina's drawing

next to her as she did it. First she drew the head, and said 'How can I do a body? I can't do it.' Then manages and drew the rest without any help. Said: 'I'm bouncing. Look, I'm turning myself around. . .like this' and began to twirl herself around.

Area of Learning: Creative

The aspects of learning shown in Amina's drawing (Figure 3.1) are: skill (in actually executing the drawing); attitude (first, not feeling confident, then gaining in confidence); knowledge and understanding (about how to represent a human in two-dimensional form, then to realise that what she had represented showed movement).

Figure 3.2 shows what some of the range of skills, attitudes, knowledge and understanding can look like for the science and technology elements of *Knowledge and Understanding of the World*.

Knowledge and Understanding of the World

ATTITUDES	SKILLS	KNOWLEDGE AND UNDERSTANDING

interest
curiosity and inquisitiveness
confidence
perseverance
concentration
openness to ideas
independence
exploring alone or with
    others
	observing
	questioning
	listening
	predicting and
	    hypothesising
	making skills (using tools
	    and materials)
	planning
	designing
	investigating skills
	estimating and measuring
	analysing and interpreting
	communicating
	evaluating
		about:
		the natural world
		living things
		forces
		light, colour and sound
		materials
		objects and systems
		how things work
		making and joining
		the local environment and
		    other relevant places
		sense of the past (in
		    relation to self and
		    family)

Fig 3.2   Knowledge and Understanding of the World: *Attitudes, Skills, and Knowledge and understanding*

Attitudes

Attitudes to learning and towards self are very important for this age group. Recently, I examined over 100 examples of 'significant achievements' for children between the ages of three and six years in order to choose approximately thirty to publish in a book on assessment (Hutchin, 1996). Almost every one of these involved some kind of change or development in *attitude*, such as confidence, persistence, independence.

Skills

Skills are also very important, as it is these which enable children to take action and to use their growing knowledge and understanding. Skills often have social or physical aspects to them. Although social development and physical development are seen as separate areas of learning in the early years, to see these as potential aspects in *any* learning, rather than just as separate areas of learning in themselves, is also useful. We can all too easily forget that an important aspect of the process of learning to write is the physical skills required, just as social skills are crucial in participating effectively in a group discussion or any group activity.

Mark *(4 years 3 months)*

Mark is in a reception class. His teacher is aware of his reluctance to write or draw and so was thrilled when an 'event' (the fish tank being knocked over) in the classroom motivated him to go independently to the writing area. He said 'It's about what happened to the fish tank.'

Area of Learning: Literacy

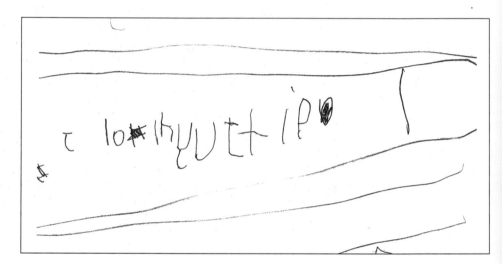

Fig 3.3
Mark's writing

This was the first time he had chosen to write, and his teacher was aware that his reluctance largely stemmed from his lack of confidence in the physical skill of writing.

Subdividing areas of learning

In the National Curriculum each subject is divided into different components or *Attainment Targets*. The National Curriculum in mathematics divides the curriculum into number, shape and space and measures (mostly to do with knowledge and understanding), whereas the skills and attitudes are addressed in the *'using and applying mathematics'* section. Seeing mathematics in this way for early years curriculum planning is also useful, as it ensures breadth across the whole area of learning.

Other areas of the curriculum also lend themselves to be organised under subheadings. *Knowledge and Understanding of the World* is made up of elements of science and technology, as well as understanding the environment and understanding about the past, elements which develop into geography and history. It is helpful to see creative development as including imaginative and role play, dance, music and art.

It may seem very complex to divide and subdivide each curriculum area in these ways, but in fact it makes the whole process of planning easier, provided we are aware that this is *not* how most learning will be *presented* to the children. We must not expect children to learn or achieve in neat little boxes like this. Learning is a messy business to which a host of personal, emotional and social factors, as well as times of day and unplanned coincidences, contribute! How often do we hear scientists say that a major breakthrough or new discovery came about as a result of coincidence or serendipity, albeit in the context of an enormous amount of carefully planned investigations and experiments.

Above all else, it must be remembered that for children of this age learning should be about *process* rather than *product* – knowing how to do something rather than necessarily getting the right answer. For example, observing a ladybird and talking about what it looks like and how it moves (the process), is more important at this age than the product – producing a drawing of it. And it is this *process* which needs to be planned for.

Long-term planning: an example

The following example of the sorts of things which could be included in long-term curriculum planning is not presented here as a substitute for an institution doing it for themselves. It is given to show the reader what long-term planning can include: it cannot replace the valuable process of doing it for yourself.

Planning for language development

Language development has been chosen for several reasons. First and foremost, like emotional, personal, social and physical development, it is an essential component in all the other areas of learning. Regardless of whether a child is able to communicate verbally or through other methods such as signing, the fact remains that language underpins so much of what we do as humans and is vital to our survival. It is *still* the most important of *all* human skills in the modern world, just as it has always been.

Yet, because speaking and listening are ephemeral and invisible, language development is often taken for granted, rather than treated as the most important part of any curriculum. Talk is often assumed to take place and rarely planned in any kind of detail, which further adds to its ephemeral nature. This lack of proper consideration only serves to undervalue it further. With the current emphasis on developing reading skills, the importance of language development in the early years in recent years has been in danger of being ignored. The National Literacy Strategy, with its daily 'Literacy Hour', concentrates on reading and writing. Yet speaking and listening are the *foundation* for development in literacy, as so much significant research has shown. This is now more clearly acknowledged in the Literacy Strategy for reception.

Research by Bryant and Bradley (1985) has shown how significant experience and knowledge of rhyme and patterns in language are for children's reading development. Wells (1986) has shown how important children's experience in creating their own stories in play is to the process of learning to read. He also notes the importance of having stories read and told. Unless a child is competent in communicating through talk (or signing), listening to talk and understanding it, then the development of literacy skills will be severely hampered.

As with any area of development, children will be on a continuum in their existing knowledge, skills, attitudes and understanding, when they first begin in nursery, playgroup or reception class settings. Some will be expressing needs and wishes by gesture and nonverbal communication, with possibly one or two word utterances going alongside these. Others will already have a huge command of language, using complex grammatical constructions and a wide vocabulary. Others may already be fluent speakers in one or two languages.

The learning intentions for speaking and listening

A full list of all the possible learning which could make up the speaking and listening curriculum would be a very lengthy document, so the list here (Figure 3.4), detailed as it is, is not comprehensive.

These learning intentions are presented under three headings: knowledge and understanding, attitudes and skills. However, four subheadings are used in the skills section, to help ensure that the

KNOWLEDGE AND UNDERSTANDING	ATTITUDES	SKILLS
To know and understand: ■ how talk works (i.e. as a two-way process); ■ that there are many different reasons for verbal communication; ■ that different situations may require different ways of speaking; ■ that different kinds of audiences may require different ways of speaking (to friends and family, to other adults and children, to younger children); ■ that there can be several ways of saying the same thing using alternative vocabulary or grammatical constructions; ■ that there are many different languages including Braille and signing; ■ that what you say can be written down; ■ an increasingly broad vocabulary; ■ a greater command of sentence structure; ■ that words can be used in playful ways to create rhymes, jokes and games; *and a* repertoire of jingles rhymes and songs which can be sung or recited.	■ to develop confidence in verbal self-expression (e.g. needs and desires, likes and dislikes); ■ to be willing to talk about events or activities the child has been involved in; ■ to develop confidence in initiating communication; ■ to develop confidence in making up and telling stories; ■ to enjoy participating in conversation with others; ■ to be willing to take risks, try out new words and new ways of saying something; ■ to persevere with giving descriptions, information, instructions to others *and* persevere with responding to those given by others; ■ to listen to and show an interest in what others have to say and develop empathy with others.	*Being able to use:* **Language for social interaction and self-expression** ■ to negotiate with others; ■ to express needs, desires, feelings and dislikes; ■ to encourage others to express their needs, desires, feelings and dislikes; ■ to participate in conversations; ■ to convey and pass on messages. **Language for thinking and reasoning** ■ to describe and give explanations; ■ to give and ask for information; ■ to recount an event or action; ■ to ask and respond to questions; ■ to reason, speculate, suggest, predict, compare, make guesses; ■ to talk about what you know. **Language for imagination** ■ to develop a storyline in play; ■ to create a story to tell to others; ■ to use talk appropriately in role play or drama; ■ to talk about imaginary ideas. **Exploring and playing with language** ■ to listen to sounds and patterns of language; ■ to play with the sounds and rhythms of language; ■ to listen to and retell rhymes and poems; ■ to create new rhymes and poems.

Fig 3.4   Learning intentions for speaking and listening

skills which enable children to use language for a range of purposes are covered appropriately and that each is given equal importance:

■ Language for social interaction and self-expression;
■ Language for thinking and reasoning;
■ Language for imagination;
■ Exploring and playing with language, and using it creatively.

Planning how to meet the learning intentions

Having dealt with the learning intentions, the next step is to look at how staff will ensure these take place, by outlining in general terms:

■ the role of the staff in supporting children's learning and development;
■ the organisation of the learning environment inside and outside to maximise learning.

The role of staff

The variety of ways in which the staff will be working with the children – the *teaching strategies* staff will use – should be part of the long-term planning. Many of these strategies will, of course, be common to each area of learning, but it can be helpful to focus on one area of learning in detail first, then to check whether there are any which would vary for other curriculum areas. The term *teaching strategies* does not mean specific activities, but the way staff interact with children in the adult-led activities and through play. The strategies listed will not need to be specific to any particular learning intentions at this stage. Discussing these strategies together as a team will be very valuable, allowing staff to make the way they work, or think they should work, explicit to each other. Once written in the long-term planning document, it can be shared with parents, managers and governors.

Examples of teaching strategies for language development might include that the staff:

■ **listen and respond** to what the children have to say or communicate, regardless of how confident and skilful the children are;
■ **talk informally and make conversation** with the children, encouraging them to talk about what interests them;

- **give a running commentary**, when appropriate, on their own or the children's actions in order to 'model' language for the children (e.g. commenting on one's own actions: *'I am stirring the paint to mix the water into the powder'*; or commenting on the child's actions in outdoor play: *'Up the steps, 1,2,3,4,5, across the bridge, into the tunnel, through the tunnel and down the slide'*);
- **communicate their intentions clearly to the children**, giving visual clues and using gesture where necessary;
- **involve themselves** in all activities and areas of provision;
- **ensure bilingual children** are in mixed groups with their English-speaking peers;
- **ensure that home languages are valued** and are seen to be valued;
- **encourage talk between children** by providing a wide range of play opportunities and activities to do together;
- **introduce new vocabulary** in contexts which are meaningful, introducing the new words relevant to what is going on at the time.

The organisation of the learning environment

Part of the role of staff is to set up a stimulating and meaningful learning environment for the children, and this forms an important part of how the curriculum is presented. Many of the learning intentions will be met, at least in part, by the play provision and activities which children can access for themselves, with or without adult support. The following areas should be provided:

- book corner;
- home corner and role play areas – in and outside;
- outdoor area, set up for many kinds of play;
- sand;
- water;
- self-help 'workshop' areas where children can draw, paint, and make 3D creations, helping themselves to the necessary tools and materials;
- small world play (on the carpet, or in the sand or water);
- block play and construction where children are able to make and play imaginatively with their creations;
- 'listening' corner with tapes and books, story props, puppets;
- interactive displays (often with a science or mathematical theme, such as collections of objects – e.g. boxes in unusual shapes, patterns, magnets);
- writing or 'office' area.

A statement should be written by the staff, clarifying how these areas are expected to be used and the kinds of learning opportunities and experiences they will provide. Many settings have done this by thinking about which learning intentions for each of the six areas of learning take place in each area of provision. One nursery centre I have worked with recently has made booklets for each area of the room and the outside area. These booklets include the possible learning intentions and the kinds of talk to encourage, as well as questions staff could ask the children, to go along with some of the learning intentions. The booklets are kept on display in the appropriate area of provision and also in the entrance for parents to see.

Showing progression

It can be useful to break down one or two learning intentions into some of the steps which may take place to show progression. Including some in the long-term planning as examples can be helpful for the medium-term and short-term planning stage. Doing this will help to ensure that *all* children are seen as being part of a continuum of learning and development. Any individual child will, of course, be at any point along the continuum of progression, and it must be remembered that children do not necessarily learn in a linear way. Children usually need to frequently revisit and practise certain skills while moving on in the acquisition of other skills at great speed. The way in which this happens will differ from child to child.

Here is an example of how progression could be shown in planning for children to be able to participate in conversations:

1 be involved in responding to a short communication (using nonverbal and gesture with some single words) with known adult;

2 be involved in initiating a short two-way communication (using nonverbal and gesture with some single words) with known adult, and listening to response;

3 be involved in longer two-way verbal communication with others beyond the immediate group of known persons;

4 participate in small group discussion on a range of topics of immediate relevance and interest;

5 participate in larger group discussion on a range of topics of immediate relevance and interest.

Doing the work: writing the long-term plan and getting it into place

Writing the long-term plans for the whole curriculum will take time, and should be spread over a manageable time scale to involve as many staff as possible. It will be time well spent, and the process of doing it is just as important as the product. Time will need to be planned and set aside for this. Initially a staff training day is often useful.

The priority in writing the long-term plans is to write up the *learning intentions* for each area of the curriculum. This will take the longest amount of time. The role of the adult and statement about the areas of provision can be a short brainstorming session which, once typed up, staff can return to, discuss and amend.

If the group decides they wish to write up their planning for each area of provision, as suggested earlier, this could be done in a series of meetings after the learning intentions have been written, delegating different areas to small working groups where possible. If the group as a whole is small in number, doing this in pairs or together as a group would be better than working alone.

When the process is completed, it can then be shared with governors or managers and parents, who can contribute before the final draft is completed. It will then only need reviewing from time to time. It can be put into action immediately and will make short- and medium-term planning so much easier.

The next two chapters look at assessment and record keeping, as once you know what learning opportunities you want the children to have, you can begin the assessment process.

Making Assessment and Record Keeping Work

4

If your assessment and record-keeping processes are to work for you, rather than you working for them, they have to be manageable and useful for planning. There are many different ways of assessing children's learning. The purpose of this chapter is to evaluate some of these methods, so that you can determine what is best for you. We have already looked briefly at some of the official requirements and recommendations on assessment (Chapter 1) and at the principles underpinning effective assessment (Chapter 2). Let us begin now by clarifying some of the terminology frequently used when talking about record keeping and assessment.

Assessment

We make an assessment on a child's learning and development when we evaluate it and make a judgment about it. It is a decision about his or her knowledge, level of understanding, skills or attitude, usually made by the staff concerned with the child. QCA (1998) states that *'Assessment reveals how far children have acquired learning'*. Mary Jane Drummond (1993) took this a step further, stating how assessment is about *seeing* children's learning, *understanding* it, then putting our understanding to *'good use'*.

The evidence for an assessment can be collected in any number of ways:

- talking to parents and carers;
- talking to the child;
- making an observation;
- listening to or participating in a conversation with the child;
- examining a sample (e.g. a drawing, a painting or some writing);
- getting a child to perform a particular task;
- administering a test.

In practice, we often make assumptions about a child. This is *not* evidence, though we often mistake it as such; neither does it provide us with any evidence itself. As Drummond *et al* (1992) point out, it is *'all too easy to make judgments based on assumptions . . . not on what children actually do'*. We need to be aware of what our assumptions are and then check whether they are right by observing the child in action.

The assessment made from an observation can tell us a number of different things – for example, about the child's learning style, interests, way of expressing him/herself, relationships with others, as well as what was learnt. It is up to us to decide what assessment to make from the evidence, based on our understanding of child development and on our knowledge of the child's previous level of learning and achievements: *' The purpose of the assessment process is to make explicit children's achievements, celebrate their achievements with them, then help them to move forward . . .'* (Hutchin, 1996).

Gathering evidence of learning and development

Let us look in more detail at how evidence of learning can be collected.

Observations

Observations involve watching the children closely and noting down what you see and hear. They may be carried out in many different ways, the most common of which are:

Timed observations

This involves observing for a specific length of time (e.g. 2 minutes or 5 minutes or longer) regardless of what the child is doing, and writing as much as possible of what is seen and heard. This is the kind of observation where you are standing back and watching, not involved directly in the activity.

Observing an area of provision or activity

This involves observing what is going on in an area of the room, outside or at a particular activity. It may involve writing down who uses the area/activity, and is likely to have an agreed focus – to look at particular aspects of development. For example, observations of the role play area could focus on how children relate to each other (social development), or the creative provision could be observed to focus on physical skills (such as how children hold pencils, brushes or scissors). Evidence of children's questioning and problem-solving techniques could be the focus of observing a science exploration activity (such as magnets) or a small group of children attempting to make dough without adult help.

Tracking observations

This involves noting down where the child goes and what they do over a period of time (e.g. 20 minutes), or at intervals over a session. It can give very useful information on the child's pattern of activities and areas of special interest, as well as, for example, how much adult interaction the child received.

Participant observations

This involves noting down what you see the children do and what you hear them say when you are working with them in any part of the setting at any time of day. Usually the notes you make will be short and quickly done.

'On the spot' or 'catch as you can' observations

This involves noting down something you see which you think is worth noting when you see it happen, whether or not you were involved with the child at the time. As with participant observations, these are quickly made jottings and notes, and should include, whenever possible, what the child actually said. Generally these will be things you feel are significant to the child and things you know you haven't previously noted, or things you want to note down because it is still happening or occurring in a new way.

The last two categories are the most useful and manageable for evidence collection over a busy session. The other methods of observing will generally only be needed in particular circumstances, such as when it has been difficult to find the evidence in any other way, or with a child who seems to spend little time near staff or is very quiet and 'just gets on with it', or because of a concern over a child for any reason. It is these other methods of observations, too, which can be so useful in monitoring and evaluating your planning, provision and practice, but in terms of records of children's learning they will be needed for *particular* purposes.

Helping to identify special educational needs

The timed observations and tracking observations will form an important part of identifying specific special educational needs in children, and so must be considered for use when you or a parent has a particular concern or worry. Often, outside agencies such as educational psychologists will suggest ways of carrying out these observations most effectively. They will need to be carefully planned and thought through, as they will require the attention of one member of staff whose time during the session will need to be devoted to the task.

Significant achievements

If something is *significant* in the context of assessment, it means it is a development or change of note. If it is an *achievement*, it means it is a step or even a leap forward, showing progress. For each child, what is significant will be different, as it depends on previous learning and what is significant for *that* child's progress. As each child progresses at a different rate, what may seem a small step for one could be a significant leap forward for another child. Significant achievements can cover a wide spectrum of learning, with a child perhaps:

- attempting something which he or she has not previously tried;
- doing something which he or she was not able to do before;
- applying new understanding, knowledge or skill in a different situation or context;
- explaining something in a new way or put into words something he or she has not previously been able to express;
- explaining how to do something to an adult or another child;
- cooperating and collaborating with others in a new way, or for a longer period of time;
- persevering for longer at an activity, either self-chosen or led by an adult.

For example (see Figures 4.1 and 4.2):

Roland *drew a snail, then he talked about the pattern on the shell and the feelers and he had another go at drawing.* **'They got things coming out – whiskers.'**

Significant achievements only show what a child *can* do, and therefore constitute progression for that child. Of course, it may be

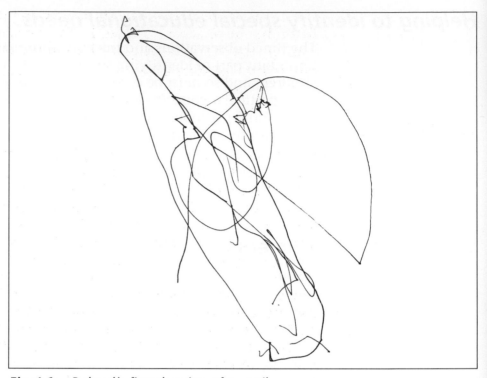

Fig 4.1   Roland's first drawing of a snail

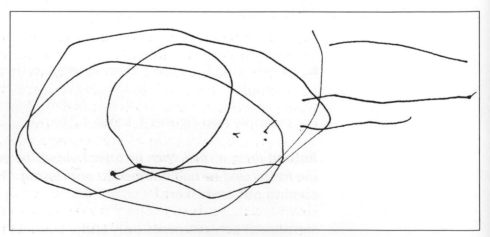

Fig 4.2   Roland's second drawing of a snail

the first time *you* notice something new and different, but not the first time the *child* has achieved it. To be realistic, no member of staff, parent or anyone else involved in the assessment process can see *everything* a child does!

Checklists

Checklists can take various forms, but they all involve a list of statements against which to assess or mark the child. They can include a mixture of visible skills, specific knowledge and concepts which can be easily checked, and occasionally broader statements about attitudes and dispositions. A child's learning is checked against the list, at certain prescribed times or ages, and can be coded, dated or highlighted as they are achieved.

There are many different forms of checklists, from a straightforward list to points on a continuum, or more attractive-looking ones designed as wheels, flowers, ladders and various other creative shapes. Many commercially produced and LEA schemes for record keeping and assessment involve some sort of checklist approach. Some expect that the evidence for checking will be gathered from observations in the normal classroom situation, rather than withdrawing and testing children, but many recommend that deliberate assessment situations are set up in the classroom. Some make no recommendations as to how to collect the evidence. Probably none would advocate that the checking was done on a 'hunch' or assumption about the child.

Records of learning and record keeping

All sorts of records on the children are kept: records of emergency contacts, addresses, parental consent for outings, information on health, and many other issues. Most of these are essential information. The *records of learning* for each child are compiled from the evidence and assessments described above, collected over time. *Record keeping* refers to these records of learning and development, the processes and systems which an institution or individual staff member puts in place for compiling records. Obviously it is much better if one system, however multi-faceted, has been agreed and is being implemented by all staff concerned. However, in a primary school it may be better to have a system for nursery and reception which is different from that for other year groups. Young children are not producing 'work' to be marked as the older children do, and the learning environment is differently organised.

For schools, record keeping is a compulsory process: *'Schools are required to keep records on every child, including academic achievements, other skills and abilities and progress made in school'* (QCA, 1997). Private and voluntary nurseries and playgroups and local authority daycare provision which are inspected by Ofsted are also expected to keep records of learning.

Assessment and record keeping in practice

All of the examples of children and their learning used in this book have been taken from children's records in a variety of settings. In each case, the evidence was gathered through observations made by staff. Sometimes there were quite lengthy observations, where a member of staff stood back to watch a group of children or an individual. On other occasions, they were quick notes and 'catch as you cans' made as the member of staff participated with the children. Sometimes staff jotted down a quick note on how a child had responded to a particular adult-directed activity, and sometimes staff recorded statements from the children, as in the comments in the opening chapter. All of these methods fit within the principles of good practice outlined in Chapter 2. None were taken from checklists, because checklists are the kind of assessments which do not provide any illustrative material. This is one of the major problems about checklists – there is no way of knowing how the assessment was arrived at or in what context, if any, it was seen to happen.

But, is it a tall order to have a detailed record on each child, built up over time, which involves observing the child in a range of situations? We need to investigate further the checklist approach. Will different approaches to assessment and record keeping lead to different outcomes for the children?

Different practices, different outcomes?

Much official advice (including the 1996 *Desirable Outcomes* document), as well as early years specialists and researchers, advocate that assessment and records should be based on observation. However, many commercial and even LEA record-keeping and assessment schemes provide a very different approach, with checklists and 'worksheets' (sometimes called *assessment materials*, *activities* or *activity sheets*). Often these involve children in colouring in the required bits or drawing a particular picture, or copying some writing. They tend to be popular, because staff feel they will be quick to do and easy to manage, with a group of children doing them all at the same time. They also ensure that every child is assessed in exactly the same way and that the same things are assessed for all.

However, we need to consider this further. In the case of activity sheets or worksheets, will they actually result in any useful evidence of children's learning beyond the child's physical ability in pencil control and hand-eye coordination? And, if an assessment task or situation is set up, will it really tell us anything beyond how the child coped with the situation or how confident the child is? If the answer to these questions is *No*, was it the intention just to assess these aspects of learning and nothing more?

Bartholomew and Bruce (1996) give a useful account of how different assessment and record keeping processes come from historically different educational traditions. They also point out that *'record keeping is an integral part of our whole approach to working with young children. . .it cannot be split off from everything else we do.'* They recount Sylva and Moore's research, which found that different types of nursery practice affected the kinds of record-keeping processes used. 'Tightly structured', formal nurseries tended to use checklists, whilst more informal nurseries used the more 'narrative' type of records based on observations (Bartholomew and Bruce, 1996).

When carried out at regular intervals, checklists are intended to show progress over time. One scheme, for example, promotes its system as *'a very simple and straightforward way to record children's achievements'* and goes on to suggest that it *'enables an accurate record to be kept for each child'* (*Sound Learning*, 1997). It recommends that the checklist can be used monthly or every three months, and that the lists are completed on the basis of the observations staff make as they work with children in their directed activities, as well as including some worksheets to be completed. Another scheme with a *'user friendly'* approach, suggests that the assessment checklists for each child should be *'updated at least once a week'* and has a column for every month. Every statement listed will need to be observed four times before it can be marked off as achieved by the child (*Core Basics*, 1997).

If the observations are written down, rather than just noted mentally, these sorts of systems will probably be much more time-consuming than any observational framework where an assessment is made directly from the observation itself, rather than against a list of predetermined statements which may not fit. Let us compare some assessments made directly from observations with using checklists.

Christopher (aged 3 years 9 months) wrote his name and his friend's name in the hairdressers' appointment book using some letter-type shapes (mainly like Cs) and zigzags, as he was playing with a group of children in the role play area. This was the first time he had attempted to write anything and he is a child who never comes to writing activities set up by staff or uses the 'self-service' writing areas in the nursery. The member of staff who had noticed this talked to him about it after the play was finished. She told him it was the first time she had seen him write and he walked off with a beaming smile, showing how pleased he was too. This was the start of something new for Christopher, as he incorporated writing and drawing into his play more and more from then on.

Answering the assessment question *'What does this tell us about Christopher's understanding of the writing process and development of writing skills?'*, would show that Christopher:

- shows understanding that writing is done for a purpose (booking appointments);
- knows that writing in this form is written as a list;
- in a play situation, is confident to try out writing for himself;
- is able to form some letter shapes as separate symbols (C);
- uses zigzag to represent writing;
- has directionality (on this occasion) left to right.

Yet, comparing this information to statements on several checklists, I found that the only information this could be checked against was *'writes own first name'* (which would be recorded as a negative response) or statements about enjoying making marks or enjoying pretend writing. None of these in any way express the vital information the staff member was able to gain about Christopher's level of understanding, his knowledge, attitude or skills by directly analysing the observation, so useful for planning purposes.

Malik, whose second language is English, was playing with magnets when a member of staff joined him. 'Look' he said, pointing to the metal ball which had attached itself to the magnet. 'That don't fall. He doesn't want to fall.' When asked why he thought this happened, he said: 'The magnet is sticky and the ball is sticky'. Staff member: 'Like glue, you mean?' Malik: 'No, like a balloon. You rub it on your leg and it sticks. I saw that on telly . . . on the cartoon . . . it was good.'

This observation shows an attempt at an explanation of his quite sophisticated hypothesis of how magnetism works. Whether technically right or not, Malik was trying to explain how magnets stick like static electricity, although he did not have the terminology in his vocabulary.

Occasionally a checklist which details scientific knowledge under *Knowledge and Understanding of the World* might contain a statement about magnetism, such as *'knows that magnets attract some materials, but not others'*, but this does not acknowledge the complex concepts which Malik is grappling with. Turning next to the language section to see if there was a statement which would better fit what Malik was doing, typical statements are *'Can talk about own experiences'*, or *'Can participate in conversations'*. Yet again, these inadequately reflect what this child was attempting to explain in his second language.

Are checklists effective in assessing learning and development?

So, checklists may seem to provide an easy-to-use system, but will the information gathered by checking the child regularly against a checklist be useful? Do checklists really record significant achievements, or just mark children off against pre-determined lists of skills that *may* be an achievement for the child or that the child may have been able to do for some time? As every child is checked off against the same list, it is only capable of giving a picture of what is considered important by the adult who devised it. It gives no holistic picture of the individual child, what the child excels at or needs most help with. An assessment system based on checklists alone cannot help staff to make planning responsive to the children's needs and strengths. A checklist may provide a summary against the list of skills which the staff feel are important for children to attain, but it would be a very crude system on which to base planning.

The list of points in Chapter 2 on what constitutes effective assessment can be used as criteria for evaluating an approach to assessment. Evaluating a checklist approach in this way will reveal the following:

Are checklists based on what the child *can* rather than *can't* do?

Checklists may highlight what a child *cannot* do and what a child *can* do. This means they are not always positive. They are likely to be too generalised to document the child's personal achievements. In areas which are marked against the checklist as *'cannot do'*, no further information on how to help the child, based on the child's interests or areas of development where the child is most confident, is available.

Do parents contribute?

It will be unlikely for parents' contributions to appear on a checklist when the assessment exercises used are carried out in the setting.

Is the child involved?

The child is unlikely to be involved through a process of self-assessment and there is not usually any space in which to record a child's own comments.

Are parents and children the starting point for the record?

No, it is the predetermined list of skills which is the starting point.

Are observations part of the daily routine? Is the child observed in action over a breadth of experiences?

Although observing the child may be recommended, what an observation shows will not be recorded unless it happens to feature on the checklist, as indicated above.

Does the record show significant developments?

There is usually no way of knowing whether the statements ticked on the checklist constitute significant developments or not. As each point in the list is a prewritten statement to tick or cross, there is no way of noting which was significant to the child's development at the time.

Can the information gathered be used for planning purposes?

Checklists are difficult to use for planning, because it is difficult to extract information which shows what would be the right thing to do *next* for the child, except in a very generalised form. This means some children could be 'coasting' rather than being given challenging learning experiences, and to others some of the planned activities might not be presented in a meaningful way.

Is it a manageable system?

The checklist system may look easy to manage, but unless the information is useful in a formative way, it will not give the kind of help which will genuinely inform teaching and working with the child.

Checklists do fulfil some of the criteria from the list in Chapter 2. First, as with any record, the information can be used to feed into *baseline assessment*. Second, parents are often asked to complete an 'entry' checklist and can thus be involved in giving information at the outset, even though it is the predetermined list of skills, rather than the information which the parents may want to give, which is the starting point. Third, checklists can be shared with parents but they are difficult to share with the child, or for the child to be involved in discussing them.

Checklists tend to result in bland and sometimes superficial information about a child, rather than showing an in-depth understanding and knowledge of how the child is really progressing. For example, a typical checklist statement under *Personal, Social and Emotional Development* might be *'plays with other children'* or *'can share and take turns'*. This gives no information about the process a child went through, or how the development took place.

Although some checklists give a space for comment, the space is usually small. A checklist approach is not sophisticated enough to enable the staff to plan effectively and it will not tell you in which situations the child is functioning best, nor anything about his or her learning style.

Different assessment situations: do they make a difference?

Children, like adults, 'perform' better in situations where they feel at ease, confident and in control, than when they are unsure of what is expected or are in an unfamiliar situation. This is why most advice on using checklists and assessment tasks states that, for young children, whenever possible they should be carried out in a familiar and non-formal setting.

Margaret Donaldson's (1978) research into some of Piaget's most well known tests has shown how children perform at a much higher level of attainment when the context and the task are made relevant to their life experiences. Bartholomew and Bruce (1996) write about Navarra's study of his own child's development of scientific concepts. Navarra concluded that it was through observing his child's play that he gained most insight to the child's conceptual development and that when the child was required to perform by answering direct questions (*'put on the spot'*, as Navarra puts it) this usually resulted in superficial replies.

We need to be aware that the circumstances in which we assess a child can greatly affect the results. Any activity which we do to assess several children in the group can meet with a host of individual responses because of the context, especially the *social* context, rather than the task itself.

Francesca joined a group of children at an adult-initiated activity set up to investigate properties of magnets. The member of staff had decided to note down in writing how each child approached the investigation, their problem-solving and investigative skills, such as observing and predicting. Francesca's friends were keen to join in and participated fully in predicting, showing their growing knowledge about magnets. Francesca, however, had little to say, made wild guesses when asked, showed little interest and then left the activity. The member of staff realised that this did not necessarily reflect Francesca's ability or understanding, but noted in her record: 'F. joined in for social reasons . . . and left half way through.' *This was one of several observations of children's responses to investigations and so she added:* 'Observe another time or in another type of investigation, especially sand', *knowing that sand play was of particular interest and the skills of observing, describing and predicting will be obvious in other situations.*

We all need to be aware, just as Navarra concluded and as the member of staff in Francesca's case was, that any kind of assessment which is not based in observing a self-chosen activity may not produce the best outcome from the child.

The 'Do one for me' or 'Do one for your record' approach

How often do we find ourselves in this situation, of trying to fill a gap in a child's record! Here are some examples of typical situations which can lead to quite different results for the children.

*Earlier in the day, **Rasel**, a child who rarely ever chose to draw or paint, had made a representational drawing of himself but was insisting on taking it home and the photocopier was broken. A staff member begged him to do another one for his record. But, although he talked a great deal in his second language (English) about what he intended to draw, all he did was to carefully strip the paper of the wax crayon he had chosen to draw with, laid it on its side and rubbed it all over the paper, saying '**Look, I'm rubbing now.**' If this second occasion had been one of the only assessment tasks in that period of time on his ability to draw representationally (such as in the many systems which ask children to draw themselves or a person), the record might show that he could not, especially if the previous drawing had not been observed in the busy nursery day (see Figs 4.3 and 4.4).*

__Bella__, on the other hand, frequently chose to draw, write, paint and make her own creations out of reclaimed materials. She had already been busily involved in the set activity for $\frac{3}{4}$ hour when her teacher asked her to 'do one more for me'. She did this willingly and the product was just as well executed and as colourful as the others she had done. Later, however, after she had been involved in a storytelling session with puppets, she was asked to draw some pictures to go with the children's stories so that staff could make a book for all the children. However, Bella soon lost interest, and began to make a little book for herself instead, copying words and pictures from a nearby book, totally unrelated to the story telling. Her story, then, could not be included in the class book on that occasion. Had this been a planned assessment task, how would she have scored?

These examples show the need for a broad spectrum of assessments to be made on children at this age across a wide range of self-initiated and adult-initiated activities if we are genuinely to assess a

Fig 4.3
Rasel's first drawing

Fig 4.4
Rasel's second drawing

child's ability. One-off assessments and checklists on adult-initiated tasks will not tell the whole story about the child, even if they are frequently repeated. For some children they may not even tell us a small portion of the story.

How to get the best from assessment practice

The key purpose of an assessment is to put the information gathered to *'good use'* – in other words, to use the information for planning. For the planning to work, we need to get the fullest and most accurate picture of a child's learning and development possible. We also have a duty to the child to do this. To do it well, a broad spectrum of evidence and opportunities for assessment *must* be provided. This means collecting assessment evidence in a variety of ways:

'On the hoof' evidence

These are the 'on the spot' or 'catch as you can' type observations and participant observations discussed earlier, which will need to be dated and a quick note added as to the context or situation in which they occurred. As far as possible, these need only focus on what are significant developments or on what you think might be significant.

It is these, together with any samples you collect, which should be the bulk of your evidence for assessments and for your records. Writing quick, short notes on self-adhesive labels or post-it notes can be the most helpful and manageable way of writing down these types of observations, as they can be easily transferred into the records.

Longer observations

This means where a member of staff has taken a few minutes to stand back and observe a child or group of children in self-initiated activities. This could be done spontaneously, because you notice something new you wish to record, or it could be planned for a particular reason (see Chapter 5).

Samples

Examples of children 'in the process of learning', as well as products such as writing, drawing, painting or a photo of a 3D model, provide very valuable sources of evidence. A sample of a *process* rather than product would show the particular skills a child used. For example, in a photo of a child making a model, the inventive way in which a child might have joined materials could be shown. Another option is to write down children's talk when they are describing what they have been doing or how they might solve a problem.

Parents

Asking parents to contribute information on what their child may be doing at home and on any achievements noted has many advantages for building a clear picture of the child's development. It also helps to build a closer partnership with parents, as well as to deepen both the staff's and parents' understanding of the child. Parents can be encouraged to bring in things their child has made or drawings done at home, and these can be added to the record.

Children

Talking to the children about themselves and their thinking, their ideas and their own views of their learning means that the child is involved in a self-assessment process.

In the next chapter we will look in detail at devising a manageable and flexible system for organising assessments and records based on this broad spectrum of evidence and assessment opportunities, and how to use these to feed into planning. Before we leave this chapter, however, if there is to be no checklist or assessment task (which always have set criteria against which to assess the child), how will staff know what to assess and what to look for?

To help staff in their observations, the following prompts on what to look for are presented for each area of learning. For each, they show the broad span of development and learning. Unlike a checklist, it is not envisaged that each prompt will be observed for every child. Rather, staff will need to decide for every child what they want to look for – what is essential to record (bearing in mind what inspectors will be looking for) and what they might record if they see it happen. The essential aspect of any assessment and record keeping is that the achievements noted are used to plan the *'what next'* for all the children in the group. How to ensure this happens is the subject matter of the chapters which follow.

What to look for

Personal, Social and Emotional Development

Collect evidence about:
- developing relationships with children and adults, e.g. how the child responds to and approaches others, participates in play and group activities;
- ability to share and take turns;
- expressing feelings, awareness of others' needs and empathising;
- growing awareness of self, and own identity;
- developing self-confidence, independence, self-control;
- ability to organise own time and make choices;
- growing awareness of own culture and those of others;
- sense of justice and responsibility.

Physical Development

Collect evidence about the child's fine and gross motor skills:
- developing manipulative skills in holding and using a range of tools: graphic tools, such as pencils, pens, paintbrushes, scissors, woodwork tools, construction sets;
- confidence in using these tools;
- developing coordination and control in moving and balancing (walking, running, climbing, using wheel toys, ball skills such as throwing, catching, hitting with bat and kicking).

Language and Literacy

Collect evidence about:

Speaking and listening
- developing ability to express needs, feelings, desires, relating experiences, expressing points of view;
- participating in talk, listening to and interacting with others (children and/or adults) in pairs, small groups and larger groups in play and role play, activities and conversations;
- using language for an increasing range of purposes such as asking and answering questions, giving information, describing, making plans and solving problems, and negotiating with others;
- participating in storytelling, rhymes and songs.

Reading

- enjoyment of being read to, looking at books, and any particular favourite books;
- interest in and awareness of print in the environment;
- 'reading-like' behaviour and reading skills (using 'book language', print direction, recognition of own name, letters, words and symbols, 1:1 correspondence between spoken and written word, association between sounds and letter, or combination of letters).

Writing

- developing awareness of some of the purposes for writing;
- being and becoming a writer, using writing in a variety of contexts – in play and for real purposes, e.g. to convey messages, write stories, etc;
- using writing-like marks, patterns and symbols to write;
- moving on to forming (some) letters (state which, in the early stages) and writing own name, some other words;
- awareness of print direction, differences between (some) upper and lower case letters.

Mathematical Development

Collect evidence about:

- using mathematical skills and ideas in everyday contexts such as play, and problem solving;
- developing awareness, understanding and use of number – 1:1 correspondence, knowing number names and sequence up to. . ., counting, comparing sets, awareness of *more* and *less*, beginning to add or take away using objects;
- developing awareness, understanding and use of shape and space: properties of some 2 and 3D shapes, identifying, describing, comparing and naming shapes in a range of contexts, using shapes to make patterns, build and construct with;
- developing awareness, understanding and use of measure: comparing size, quantity, time, speed; using appropriate language of measure such as *more, less, full, empty, half full, longer, shorter*, etc;
- developing mathematical language and vocabulary in all the above, particularly about position, quantity, comparisons and differences.

Knowledge and Understanding of the World

Collect evidence about:

Science and technology

- developing interest in and curiosity about the physical world and living things, and talking about this;
- developing skills in observing, asking questions, predicting, suggesting reasons, experimenting and investigating, talking about what has been observed or done;
- developing an interest in and enjoying making and constructing, using a range of materials (wooden blocks, construction sets, reclaimed materials);
- experimenting and persevering with joining and fixing;
- developing an interest in and talking about how things work;
- developing 'making' skills and moving towards planning and designing before making;
- talking about all of the above.

The past and the local environment (beginnings of historical and geographical understanding)

- developing interest in and awareness of the past in relation to self and family – interest in and awareness of the local environment and some of its features;
- interest in and awareness of other parts of the world, relevant to the child's own experience or gained through other sources.

Creative Development

Collect evidence about:
- enjoyment of and involvement in imaginative play and role play; ability to develop and sustain a storyline during the play, alone or with others;
- enjoyment of and involvement in drawing, painting, collage, modelling, using malleable materials;
- developing representational skills and pattern-making, awareness of colour and texture;
- talking about own creations and those of others;
- enjoyment of and involvement in music, dance and movement, noticing and creating patterns; listening or watching and responding.

Summing up

To sum up the discussions in this chapter, it will be helpful to look at how the recommended system for collecting evidence of learning and achievements can be of benefit to all involved. Records which are made up of a range of evidence – based on using observation techniques across the full breadth of learning opportunities and experiences, provided inside and outside – can:

. . . benefit staff by:

■ helping to show what progress and development over time can look like and how this can differ from one child to another;
■ helping staff to evaluate their role in this;
■ being an aid to planning;
■ helping staff in talking to parents about their child;
■ raising staff awareness of the potential of the provision they make available to children.

. . . benefit the child by:

■ being known better by the staff;
■ staff noticing what the child can do and where he or she needs support;
■ raising staff expectations: observations in a range of different situations often show that the child is more capable than was thought;
■ better planning for the next step in the child's learning;
■ developing his or her own awareness of achievements, through involvement in the assessment process.

. . . benefit the parents by:

■ showing them their own child's progress ;
■ becoming more involved in talking to staff about their child's learning;
■ seeing the work of the setting in action;
■ enabling them to find out more about how children learn.

. . . benefit the institution by:

■ informing parents better about what the nursery/playgroup/class does;
■ monitoring and evaluating provision through reviewing the records of the children.

Some of these benefits and purposes are secondary to the main purpose of finding out about and documenting the child's learning, but are nevertheless useful too. A record-keeping system which works well should be able to fulfil these purposes and still be manageable for the staff. The next chapter will look at devising a system for record keeping and assessment, involving parents and the children in order to help you.

Looking at Children Learning 5

The previous chapter recommended a system for record keeping where evidence of learning is collected through a variety of observational methods. Using this evidence to assess the child and tease out what could be offered to the child next, means putting the evidence to *'good use'*, as recommended by Drummond (1993). It means *using* the information gathered for planning purposes – to fulfil needs and set up challenging learning opportunities for children.

This chapter looks at the detail of this assessment and record-keeping system, starting from the initial stage of talking to parents about their children before or on admission to your setting or class. Next, examples of observations and notes on children's achievements show the evidence-collecting process in action, in a range of settings. Effective ways of involving the children in the assessment process are then discussed, and finally we look at how to set up the record-keeping system.

Right at the start: gathering information from parents and carers

The starting point for any child's record should be information from the person or people who know the child best – usually the parents. Most nurseries, playgroups and primary schools collect information from parents for their admission forms, but this does not always include questions about the child's interests or general development. Sometimes this information stays in an admissions file rather than being shared with the staff actually working with the child.

Finding out about children from their parents helps staff to get to know them and begin compiling the records. The information collected should be useful and be used to feed planning, not just completed and put away. It should include information on how parents think their children might settle, how confident the children usually are with other adults and children, special interests and favourite kinds of play and activities, as well as the parents' views on their child's development. This will help with planning for the 'settling in' period, as staff can then provide some things for children to do which are both familiar and support their interests. There will be some similarities between one child's needs and interests and those of others in the group, so planning for one will involve planning for several children.

The questions in the panel on the next page, compiled from many discussions with staff from a wide range of settings, provide examples of the kind of information to collect from parents.

When and how to get the information

A reception class with 30 children to admit in the first few days or weeks of term poses very different circumstances to a small playgroup, so when and how to talk to parents and gather this kind of information needs to be appropriate to what is realistically possible. Every institution should make a time for parents to meet with the staff before their child starts, preferably individually, although small group meetings would be better than trying to meet all new parents together. There are several ways of getting to know children and their parents which different settings may use:

- **Home visits** – a time for a member of staff to meet the child and other family members. As the focus of the visit is to introduce the staff member to the child, it may not be the best time to 'interview' the parent, but many parents will be happy to complete a form afterwards, once it has been explained.
- **A visit to the setting** – before the child starts, where each new child and their parents visit at a different time so that there is time to meet with the staff. In order to discuss the information required from parents, time will need to be set aside for the staff members concerned to talk with the parent.
- **A meeting for parents and their children before they start** – in small groups would be better than all together.
- **During the first few days, while parents are staying to 'settle in' their child** – often this can be a good time, as both staff and parents are together over a longer period of time and are focusing together on settling the child in.

How the information from parents is gathered is best kept flexible, so that it can be tailored to the family concerned. Many parents

Child's Name:

Date of Birth:

Date of Entry: *Age at entry:*

Languages spoken at home:

- *Names of other family members and other significant people close to child:*

- *Any previous experience of nursery or playgroup:*

- *Does your child have any particular play interests at the moment, or particular toys she/he likes to play with?*

- *What other sort of things does your child show interest in or talk about?*

- *Is your child used to playing with other children and does he/she enjoy this?*

- *How does he/she respond to situations and people who are new to him/her?*

- *Do you think your child's language development is proceeding well?*

- *Does your child enjoy books and listening to stories? Does he/she have any favourite rhymes, stories, videos or tapes?*

- *Does your child enjoy and get involved in imaginative type play and/or activities such as drawing, painting, counting, building or constructing?*

- *Do you feel his/her physical development is what you would expect for his/her age? If you have a garden which your child can play in or when you go to the park, what does your child like to do?*

- *What do you expect he/she will like about the nursery/playgroup/school?*

- *Is there any more information you would like to know about the nursery/playgroup/school and what your child will be doing?*

- *Do you have any concerns or worries about your child's development?*

- *Is there any other information you would like us to know in order to help your child settle and be happy ?*

may not feel confident to complete a form themselves, or are too busy to do so. The best approach will be to have a list of prompts or questions, like the one shown in the panel, for staff either to ask parents in a discussion or interview, or for parents to complete in their own time. For some parents, where there is no shared language between staff and parents, an interpreter will be necessary, but where this is not possible a great deal of mutual understanding can be arrived at by ensuring a relaxed setting, such as on a home visit with enough time allowed for communication to flow.

The next section looks at examples of children's learning which form the ongoing records of achievements, with examples from parents showing how they have been involved in a continuing way with the record-keeping process. This is easier to do with some parents than others, and can be particularly difficult with working parents. Because of this, some settings have a system for communicating with working parents, such as a home-school link diary which the staff or the parent can use when they wish to, or on a regular weekly or monthly basis; others have set times when parents can telephone, as well as the usual open evenings and meetings. Bearing in mind that *partnership* with young children's parents is vital to their education, contact with all parents will need to be accommodated.

Collecting the evidence

Chapter 4 explored the most useful ways of collecting observational evidence on children's learning. Let us now look at how this works in practice, with some real examples of learning and development which have been collected in a range of settings. Every example is about a different child, illustrating the range of possible significant developments children make which could be recorded. Records need to show how the child is changing and developing over time, so they need to be compiled over the whole of the child's time in the setting or class. As the booklet *Looking at Children's Learning* (SCAA, 1997) states:

❛ *A child's response during a single activity is not always an accurate or reliable guide to underlying competence. Therefore there needs to be caution about conclusions drawn on the basis of one activity alone.* ❜

When any note is made about a child's learning – whether an observation of play, a note made in passing as a child was seen to do something they had not done before, or a participant observation at a staff-led activity – the staff will need to decide what this tells them about the child. This should be written down at the time and, whenever possible, followed by a suggestion for possible future planning. This kind of planning can cover a wide range of possibilities, such as continuing to provide similar opportunities for the child, or for staff to take a more 'proactive' line. Each of the examples which follow are presented in the same format:

1 Evidence (example or observation)

2 Area of learning

3 What does it tell us about this child's learning and development?

4 Implications for planning

The examples are divided into the categories of evidence recommended in Chapter 4:

- participant observations, catch as you can's, and notes on significant achievements;
- longer observations;
- observations from parents;
- samples;
- conversations with children.

Participant observations, and 'catch as you can' type observations and notes on significant achievements

Sarah *(3 years 9 months)*

Evidence (example or observation)
Used mosaic shapes to make a pattern, starting by filling up edges along each side, then filling in the centre. Brought it to show member of staff.

Area of learning: *Personal, social and emotional and Mathematical development.*

What does it tell us about this child's learning and development?
Persevered with self-chosen activity until completed without help. Proud
of her achievement and first time she has wanted to show it to staff.
When asked how she managed to complete it alone, she said 'Because I
ate a lot.'

Implications for planning
Encourage her to talk to staff about what she has been doing.
Encourage her to try pattern-making again.

Robert (4 years 4 months)

Evidence (example or observation)
When tidying up the home corner, noticed the silhouettes for the cups
on the shelf and that some cups were missing. Knew without counting
that three were missing and when one was found, said 'We still need
to find two.'

Area of learning: Mathematical development

What does it tell us about this child's learning and development?
Able to work out number of items missing through mental
addition/subtraction with four items. First time this development has
been noticed by staff.

Implications for planning
Give him more opportunities to work out addition and subtraction,
both with objects and without, using small numbers in a wide range of
situations (i.e. making up games at group times, as well as in self-
chosen activities and play). Make sure all staff know about his skills in
this.

Laura (4 years)

Evidence (example or observation)
Wrote line of writing-like marks, first line left to right and second line
right to left. Staff member asked her if she was writing. Laura: 'Yes I'm
writing'. Staff: 'What does it say?' Laura: 'I don't know. I haven't
decided yet.'

Area of learning: Literacy (writing)

What does it tell us about this child's learning and development?
Skills observed: some idea of direction of print in English, but not
always correct. Has idea that writing conveys a message, but does she
know that you have to think of message first before you write?

Implications for planning
Continue to provide her with lots of models of writing and adults
writing in different contexts – such as group writing where staff member
scribes on large paper, as well as in less formal situations. Continue to

talk to her about her writing, pointing out the features she uses, as appropriate, and asking her what it might say.

Darren *(3 years 6 months)*

Evidence (example or observation)
Making a collage picture as a member of staff joined him. Began to talk about his family. 'Wrote' his name on his picture for the first time.
Area of learning: *Language and Literacy*
What does it tell us about this child's learning and development?
Rarely joins in conversation with adults or other children. First time he has attempted to write his name.
Implications for planning
Adult to spend more time with him, joining him once he has settled to an activity himself, engaging him in informal conversation. Encourage him to write his name on all he does himself, and remind him that he can do it.

Julian *(4 years 9 months)*

Julian is a child with special educational needs, particularly with regard to playing and interacting with others.
Evidence (example or observation)
Julian was alone at the water tray when three others joined. He continued to play. Short talk with Alex, telling Alex his name: 'I'm Julian Jameson.' Alex: 'And I'm Alex Morgan.' Julian: 'I'm not Julian Morgan, I'm Julian Jameson.'
Area of learning: *Personal, social and emotional and Language development*
What does it tell us about this child's learning and development?
First time Julian has ever been seen at nursery to stay when others join an activity, or to interact in this way.
Implications for planning
Try to replicate situation. Classroom was very quiet as many children were outside, so use time of day when classroom is quiet. Staff to stand back and watch, not to get involved yet.

Anna *(5 years)*

Evidence (example or observation)
Chose to use the writing area with a friend. Began to make a fan. Another child joined and asked her what she was doing. Staff member asked her if she could show others how to make a fan. 'I'll show you. . .you go this way first, then like that and then you smooth it

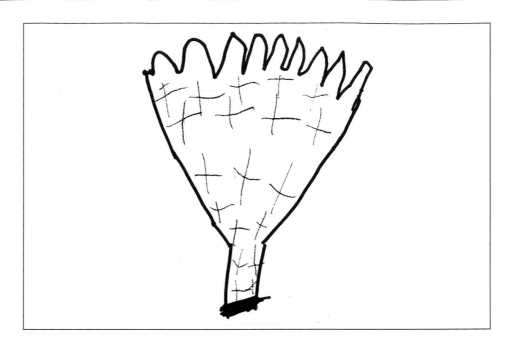

Fig 5.1
Anna's fan drawing

down like this.' *As others were unsure, she offered to draw a picture of how to do it.*
Area of learning: *Creative development (and Technology)*
What does it tell us about this child's learning and development?
Able to teach others skills in making, and to represent her model through drawing
Implications for planning
Encourage her to share her skills to teach others what she knows more often.

Longer observations

When a concern about a child is raised, or the staff have highlighted the need for a closer observation as they feel they may not be planning appropriately for a child or do not feel they know the child well enough, it may be important to plan to do a longer and more detailed observation. Here is an example.

Michael *(4 years) is a child who is very quiet and reticent when around adults and spends much of his time in the outdoor area involved in physical games such as football. The staff decided a tracking* *observation was needed to find out what he did over a period of time (15 minutes). The pattern of his activity during this time was noted and analysed.*

This showed that he spent some of this time waiting for or following another child (including a few seconds drawing while waiting for the other to finish) but when they finally settled to an activity he became deeply involved in imaginative play, developing a story with the other child, using playpeople and cars.

The observation had been useful as it showed that although he did not take the lead in making decisions about what to do, once involved he was able to take an equal part in constructing the play storyline.

Implications for planning
It was decided that staff should spend more time with him in activities once he had settled, to get him to feel more relaxed with them, before encouraging him to persevere in areas such as drawing.

Observations from parents

Grace *(3 years)*

Evidence (example or observation)
(Written by grandmother) Grace wanted me to take her to the bookshop and then on to the park. She wrote a shopping list, then drew a map of how to get from my house to the park. As she handed me the shopping list she said : 'That's to put in the shopping trolley.'
Area of learning: *Literacy and Knowledge and Understanding of the World*
What does it tell us about this child's learning and development?
Understands purpose of writing and making writing like marks. Knows a map can represent a journey (walk to park).
Implications for planning
Encourage her to use writing in her play. Involve her in map making – e.g. how to get to playgroup, how to get around the building and outside area.

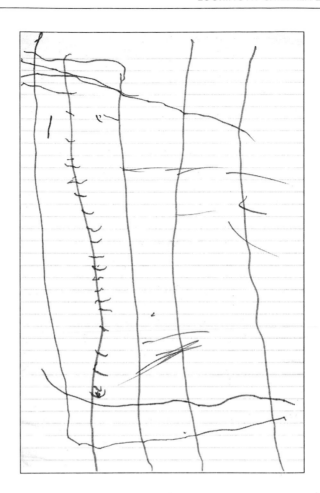

Fig 5.2
Grace's map: how to get to the park

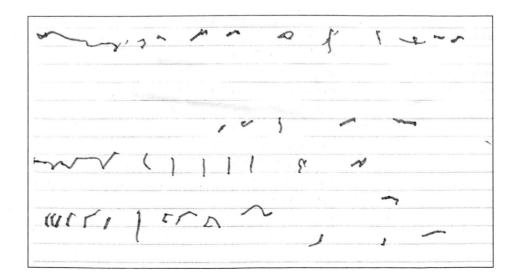

Fig 5.3
Grace's shopping list

Charlie *(4 years 11 months)*

Evidence (example or observation)
Member of staff leaving nursery at the same time as parent and child noticed the game they were playing – he walked ahead very fast and counted his footsteps as he got ahead. Counted to twenty-nine, then said twenty-ten, twenty-eleven, and did the same at forty and fifty. Parent and staff helped him get it right.
Area of learning: Mathematical development
What does it tell us about this child's learning and development?
Staff had no idea he could count to such high numbers and are now aware of what help he needs to move on.
Implications for planning
Staff to involve him in lots of counting activities with high numbers, and reinforce the number sequence after 29, 39, 49, 59.

Conversations with children

Luciana *(3 years 11 months)*

Evidence (example or observation)
Talking to L today about speaking Portuguese. 'No, I speak English and Susan (childminder) speaks English too. I speak only English here.' Later on she told me: 'I speak Portuguese with my mum. She says "Obrigada" and I say "Obrigada" too.'
Area of learning: Language and Personal, social and emotional development
What does it tell us about this child's learning and development?
L's first language is Portuguese and she has been learning English since she was two years old. The conversation shows how aware she is about when it is appropriate to use which language.
Implications for planning
Staff to make some signs and notices for wall displays with L and her mum's help in Portuguese. Do this too with other bilingual children to raise the status of their first languages. Talk about languages with all the children at group time.

Chantalle *(4 years 6 months)*

Evidence (example or observation)
A display of old and new objects had been put up in the classroom. Chantalle in conversation with a staff member about it. 'New things you buy in a shop.' Staff: 'And what about the old things?' 'There was nothing so you couldn't buy things. They had to make their

own things and build their own houses. . .and catch their own food.' *She also said she knew this because she had a book at home.*
Area of learning: *Knowledge and understanding of the world*
What does it tell us about this child's learning and development?
Shows a level of awareness of history the staff did not know or expect. Also showed ability in giving clear explanation to others.
Implications for planning
Plan to have more extended conversations with groups of the older children. Ask her to bring in her book to add to the display, then she can show it to others.

Samples

The comments written here could be written on the back of the sample, a post-it or paper attached to it. Each sample will need to be dated.

Aaron *(3 years 4 months)*

Evidence (example or observation)
First drawing at nursery.
Area of learning: *Creative development*
What does it tell us about this child's learning and development?
Spent time on this drawing, carefully putting marks inside circular shapes. Gave it to staff member for his record.
Implications for planning
Continue to encourage him to draw.

Fig 5.4
Aaron's drawing

Clarence *(3 years 6 months)*

Evidence (example or observation)
Writing – he said it was his name.
Area of learning: Literacy
What does it tell us about this child's learning and development?
Using writing-like shapes for some of this.
Implications for planning
Continue to encourage him to write in his play and activities.

Fig 5.5
Clarence's writing

Leon *(4 years)*

Evidence (example or observation)
Now beginning to play cooperatively with other children – here very much involved in making a model together (see Figure 5.6).
Area of learning: Personal, social and emotional development
What does it tell us about this child's learning and development?
Shows real development of social skills.
Implications for planning
Continue to encourage and congratulate him (the photo helped in illustrating his success to him).

Fig 5.6
Leon making his model

Danielle *(4 years 6 months)*

Evidence (example or observation)
Drew picture of lots of people then asked to write about it. Wrote her name (or letters from it) but then said she didn't know how to write. I suggested she had a go, then she could ask me to write it. She told me what she had written 'The little girl was in bed' and I then wrote it for her.

Area of learning: *Literacy*

What does it tell us about this child's learning and development?
First attempt at writing more than the letters from her name.

Implications for planning
Support and encourage at every opportunity.

Fig 5.7
Danielle's drawing

Fig 5.8
Danielle's writing

Husam *(4 years 4 months)*

Evidence (example or observation)
Drawing and writing inspired by a book-making session using the story Handa's Surprise, *by Eileen Browne.*
Area of learning: *Creative and Literacy development*
What does it tell us about this child's learning and development?
Drawing more detailed than before, first time he has attempted to write other than copying own name.
Implications for planning
Encourage to have a go at writing in this way again, congratulate him on his drawing.

Husam has written Handa is putting in basket.

Fig 5.9
Husam's drawing

Hameed *(4 years 6 months)*

Evidence (example or observation)
Hameed has drawn his dad and tried to write his dad's name.
Area of learning: *Creative and Literacy development*
What does it tell us about this child's learning and development?
Needs a great deal of encouragement to sit down and participate in

Fig 5.10
Hameed's drawing of his dad

group activities, so I'm really pleased with his drawing – initially very reluctant. He did this in the writing area rather than at a table.
Implications for planning
Make sure he can choose where to work and praise him when he has achieved like this.

Jerome *(4 years 11 months)*

Evidence (example or observation)
Drawing: 'This is me playing football.'
Area of learning: Creative
What does it tell us about this child's learning and development?
Able to represent movement in his drawing by the positioning of legs.
Implications for planning
Talk to him about his skills in drawing.

Fig 5.11
Jerome playing football

Kareema *(5 years)*

Evidence (example or observation)
First time has attempted to write numerals. She watched another child who was sitting next to her.
Area of learning: *Mathematical development and writing skills*
What does it tell us about this child's learning and development?
First time she felt confident enough to try something new As yet she does not speak any English, and has felt quite lacking in confidence in new environment. Helped by sitting next to this particular child.
Implications for planning
Encourage same child she was with today to be with her again – help develop friendship?

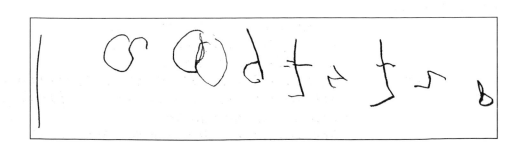

Fig 5.12
Kareema's writing

Talking with the children about their learning

Some of the examples just discussed are conversations with children which show their levels of understanding about the world around them. These conversations were significant for the staff concerned, as it helped them to understand the child better, but may not have been significant for the child. However, talking is also a vital part of an important process.

Talking to children about their learning, their ideas and their thinking, provides an opportunity for children and staff to reflect together on their knowledge and understanding. Having a conversation with a child about their own learning is a time not to be missed, yet it is not something which is regularly or frequently planned in many early years settings. Some settings, however, have developed processes to ensure it does happen.

Finding ways to talk to the children

In the *Tracking Significant Achievement* books (e.g. Hutchin, 1996) it is recommended that all children should be involved in discussing their achievements with staff, as/when they happen and are recorded. This is perhaps easier with older children, when most of what is being recorded is a result of teacher-led activities and much of it is written or represented on paper. However, slightly different strategies are required with younger children, especially when the achievements noted have taken place in a play context, or involve personal, social and emotional development. Staff working with young children have to find more creative ways to talk to children about their achievements than those working with older children.

The first step is to tell the children what you are writing; sometimes this will mean telling them afterwards, so as not to interrupt what they are doing. Invite them to add their own comments too, but do not worry if they do not respond or if they respond in a way that you did not expect (e.g. Sarah's comment *'because I ate a lot'*). The important point is that you have brought to their attention the fact that you are recording positive things you have seen them do, which you feel are achievements for them, and you have given them the opportunity to reflect and respond.

Children need to be involved at every stage in their own assessment. Here are some useful strategies:

- Tell them what you are writing.
- Tell them about their record and show it to them frequently.
- With any 'product', talk about it with them, and tell them you wish to put it, a photo or a photocopy of it in the record.
- Allow them to choose their own things to add to the record as well.
- Even if the child doesn't respond the first few times you talk to them about their achievements, don't be put off. Continue.
- Ask open-ended and inviting questions which will require more than one-word responses or yes/no answers, but don't force the child to respond.

For bilingual children, make sure you include the necessary visual support so that the child can understand what you are saying. Gesture and facial expressions to show how pleased you are can help. It may mean taking the child to show them what you saw and tell them you thought it was very good.

The best approach, and easiest to implement, is once you have some records to show, to share these regularly with the child. One nursery, for example, where each nursery worker and teacher has a 'key' group of children (for whom they are responsible in terms of

Fig 5.13
Sharing records with children

links with the family and organising records), allocates a time once a week for the key worker to spend time with children from their group – either as a whole, with individuals or small groups. This is planned in their weekly planning sheets and they ensure that some of this time is organised to share the records with the children.

Writing down a conversation with a child about their time in the class or setting

Some LEAs, such as Westminster, have produced a format – for example, a blank sheet with a few prompts at the top of the page – to record a discussion with the child. This is a lovely activity to do with children, and some nurseries ensure this happens towards the end of the time that the child is with them. The opening comments of this book were recorded in just this way. Not only does it encourage reflection, but at the same time it can reinforce the message that what is said can be written down, and help a child to understand the rules of 'dictation' (such as not talking too fast!).

Setting up the record-keeping system

All this information and evidence needs to be compiled and stored to make up a record of achievement for each child. Many LEAs and some private and voluntary education organisations concerned with young children have produced a *child profile* format. These can be very useful, and some have separate sheets for each area of the curriculum. They often include a breakdown on what to look for, similar to that in Chapter 4. Some local authority systems (e.g. Kensington and Chelsea, 1993; Westminster, 1994; Islington, 1998) place the prompt at the top of blank sheets where staff can write their observations and notes. In Westminster and Islington's versions of this format, a column beside the observation space is left for staff to add their planning possibilities resulting from the observations.

It is usually best to make up an individual record for each child, so that the record is easily accessible for the staff to share regularly with the child and parents. Many teachers have traditionally kept all their records in one folder together, but this system makes the whole recording process unwieldy and often results in staff having to spend a great deal of time sorting out records after the children have gone home. The best idea is to keep all the notes, observations and samples in a separate folder, such as a cardboard document wallet, for each child.

Whether using a folder or a profile format, each example, observation or note is added to the record as it is made. The essential thing is to have the paper and writing tools always at the ready, and not to worry about *how* something is written. Records do not need to be beautifully written in best handwriting. It is when staff feel they have to do this that problems with manageability occur. The emphasis of the record keeping must be on using the information gathered to plan the next steps for the child, not writing out observations neatly.

Notes and observations can be written directly into a profile format, on post-its, self-adhesive labels or note pads (spiral bound 'reporters' note pads can be very handy as sheets can easily be torn off). Some schools have attractively designed photocopiable sheets on different sized paper, to be used according to the amount to be written, and store these in different parts of the room so they are always to hand. An 'assessment' format similar to the one used for the examples in this chapter can be very useful, ensuring that what the child learnt and planning are thought about every time.

If records are based on observations, as in the examples shown, they will not be negative statements or personal comments which you would be unwilling to share with parents, children or other staff. Compiled in the way described above, they will also be immediately accessible as and when you need them.

Knowing what you have got

The *Tracking Significant Achievement* system recommends using a group chart or matrix to tick or date every time you have added to a child's record. The most common format is a list of children's names on one side and curriculum area headings on the other. Then, at a glance, it is possible to see what you have collected and where there are any gaps. It is not then a question of filling the gaps, but thinking about why they have occurred. Sometimes a pattern may emerge. A gap can occur in one area of learning for many of the children. Sometimes it is a question of spending time observing that area of learning more carefully, or there may be a need to set up more specific activities to address an imbalance in what is provided.

Often staff find that there are certain children they have not recorded much about. The chart or matrix will help you identify what you have already collected. Discussion between staff as to why certain children may be difficult to keep records on is useful, as together they can then think of ways to address the problem.

For example:

- If it is because a child is shy or chooses not to spend time with adults:
  spend more time with the child, working alongside them until they become more familiar.
- If it is because staff do not observe or make records about an area of provision in which this child spends a lot of time:
  plan to spend time in that area and carry out 'participant observations'.
- If staff do not seem to notice any developments or achievements:
  make a point of observing the child at play and a variety of activities, then think about whether your planning fits with the child. Are there enough challenges? Are the steps forward for this child very small and do you need to plan more specifically for him/her? Do you need to talk to the child more frequently?

Above all, it is not a question of rushing to fill gaps. There may be a need for you to observe a particular child more closely using another type of observation, such as a longer one, a tracking or timed observation. No particular time scale is suggested to add something for each child, as each individual will be different. However, staff will need to decide, for every child, what are the *essential* things to be looking out for, and what is *optional*, to record if it happens.

How can we plan from assessments?

As can be seen from the examples in this chapter, every assessment has an implication for future planning for the child concerned. This, in fact, is the main point, if not the *only* point, in assessing children – to decide the 'what next?'. A systematic process is needed to ensure that this kind of planning really does happen. Leaving it to chance in a busy classroom, nursery or playgroup, with very little time for adults to reflect, think and plan, can only mean that, with the best intentions in the world, much will be forgotten and planning will remain at the level of general provision rather than addressing specific learning needs.

The next two chapters look at this in greater detail. We first examine the medium- and short-term planning, as this is where the staff's knowledge of the children and their development fits into the planning and assessment cycle.

Planning the Detail 6

The two time-scales for planning we have not yet addressed are the *medium-term*, usually for a half term or a whole term, and the *short-term*, usually daily or weekly, planning. These are more detailed and specific than the long-term planning overview discussed in Chapter 3, specifying in advance what children will learn, and at the same time making it really relevant to these children at *this* point in time. It is the medium and short-term planning which can be the exciting part of planning, bringing long-term planning alive and making it into a reality. It is here that staff contribute their knowledge of the children and their own ideas on what these children need to move their learning forward. But in order to make medium and short-term plans effective and easy, the long-term planning must be in place.

Medium-term planning links long-term planning to what will be appropriate for the group of children as a whole over several weeks. Here staff will be acknowledging and building on the children's interests and thinking about the learning needs of the group. **Short-term planning**, on the other hand, is much more immediate and detailed, happening on a weekly and, if possible, daily basis. This is where planning responds to children's individual needs, at the same time as drawing on, and if necessary adjusting, the plans made for the medium term.

Many early years staff have found the medium-term and short-term planning difficult to get right. Some feel that having to predict in advance what might be appropriate, when children can change so rapidly, creates difficulties. They feel that an unexpected event or developing interest cannot be followed up as, for the sake of accountability, they must be doing what their plans say – and inspectors, heads and managers will be looking to see that what has been planned is in fact happening. Others feel, particularly in relation to short-term planning, that making realistic plans for all the children when there is a vast variation in their knowledge, skills and understanding is a formidable task.

But there are some very effective and quite straightforward ways of solving these problems, ensuring flexibility and catering for individuals yet still answering the call for accountability. The way through the problems is to keep the children and their learning central to the process.

Medium-term planning

The best approach to medium-term planning is to concentrate on what you want the children to learn and experience through specifying **learning intentions**, rather than the actual activities which will be offered. This helps to address many of the concerns already mentioned. The moment that *learning* becomes the central focus in the minds of the staff, the easier it is to address the need for spontaneity and flexibility to meet the needs of the children.

Sometimes staff are asked in their medium-term planning to give detailed plans of what is to be done week by week over the period. This is really the role of the *short*-term planning, however. Let us clarify the medium-term planning process.

The process

The main job for medium-term planning is to make a clear connection between long-term planning – the entitlement to learning – and the children themselves. The best way to do this is to think of both at once, by having the long-term planning to hand and looking at it in relation to what the children in your group need *now*. To do this, staff will need to put time aside to meet and make decisions on what is appropriate – an hour or so should be enough.

The process of medium-term planning requires the pooling of information from three sources:

- the long-term plans;
- the range of needs over the group of children as a whole;
- any general interests amongst the group of children you have.

The learning intentions from the long-term plan are chosen for each area of learning, appropriate to the needs of the group as a whole, based on the children's needs and interests.

The range of learning needs

The range of needs to be considered for the children concerned should prioritise personal, social and emotional development, language and literacy and mathematics, but may also include other areas such as developing imagination and creativity. Having decided what these needs are in a general way, staff will choose learning intentions which match the long-term plans. As the long-term planning gives an overview of learning, looking at the range of needs of the children in the group may mean that some of the broad learning intentions need to be broken down into smaller steps, to ensure that they address the levels of skill, attitude and understanding of the children. For example, in mathematical development, the learning intention *'understanding and responding to positional words'*, for some, may mean simple verbal instructions to act out physically; for others, it may mean creating, reading and using a map of the garden. Chapter 3 also gives examples of how learning intentions can be broken into stages.

If all the children are new, as when all children start in September once a year, then the personal knowledge the staff have of those children is limited to the information gathered from parents. This information will give staff some ideas of the children's interests, needs and strengths. For the first half term, the burning issues to be planned for will be to do with settling in, introducing children to the routines, buildings, expectations, the choices they can make and, most importantly, to other children in the group. The planning for this period will mean taking the learning intentions appropriate to these needs for the group as a whole, ensuring of course that all areas of learning are planned for.

At other times of year the staff will have a good idea of the range of needs amongst the group for most areas of learning. In settings where children are admitted over the whole year, or a few each term, the staff will usually know the majority of children well enough to have built up some records. It will then mean planning the 'induction' for some and different learning intentions for the others – who, of course, will be there to help with the 'induction' of the new children as well.

Building on children's interests and passions

Whether the children are new or not, the staff may already have a very good idea about any particular interests or consuming passions to follow up. For example, an overwhelming interest in bike play for some children could be developed to look at and create routes around the outdoor area, building obstacle courses and map making. The specific learning intentions for this theme may fall under the headings of *Knowledge and Understanding of the World* and *Mathematics*, but much physical, creative, language and literacy learning can also be planned for those children who are involved. This will, however, be just part of the medium-term planning, relating to both outdoor and indoor provision.

Developing an area of learning or type of provision

Many settings find that medium-term planning provides an ideal opportunity to develop a particular area of learning or type of provision which they feel does not currently have a strong enough focus. For example, one playgroup I visited felt that it did not develop children's understanding of how everyday things work or their thinking about what objects are made of. They decided to set up an interactive display table where children could explore an array of materials and objects, and planned for staff to spend time sitting near the display to talk with the children.

Finally, special events – often to do with the time of year, which may be relevant to the children's experiences or particular festivals – will need to be included.

Figure 6.1 shows how the medium-term planning needs to cover some of the learning intentions for each area of learning and gives some broad ideas of how the planning will be carried out.

What to include in medium-term planning

The right-hand side of the diagram shows what the medium-term planning includes: the appropriate learning intentions, with a broad outline of how these will be met. This should include some ideas on how the learning will be offered through areas of provision both inside and in the outdoor area. Some ideas for staff-led activities can also be incorporated, but these should be seen only as possibilities. The *detailed* planning of activities will need to be organised in the short-term rather than the medium-term planning, to ensure they meet the specific children's needs and interests at the actual time they will be offered. For example, to develop the children's confidence in writing for themselves may

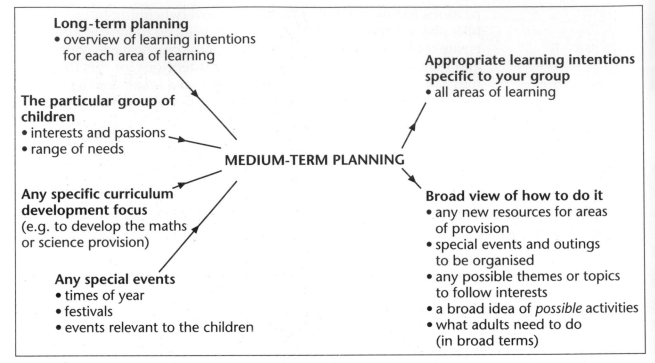

Long-term planning
• overview of learning intentions for each area of learning

Appropriate learning intentions specific to your group
• all areas of learning

The particular group of children
• interests and passions
• range of needs

MEDIUM-TERM PLANNING

Any specific curriculum development focus
(e.g. to develop the maths or science provision)

Broad view of how to do it
• any new resources for areas of provision
• special events and outings to be organised
• any possible themes or topics to follow interests
• a broad idea of *possible* activities
• what adults need to do (in broad terms)

Any special events
• times of year
• festivals
• events relevant to the children

Fig 6.1   Medium-term planning

mean making books with some children and involving writing in role play to accommodate others. These two ideas can be entered into the medium-term plan. The specific details (i.e. the content and form of the books, or developing role play into a garage or hospital, say) will be left to the short-term plans.

Resources to be collected in advance – such as library books, materials for celebrating a particular event or festival, tanks for minibeasts or local maps for the interest in routes – will need to be considered. Special events or outings will also need to be arranged. Staff should discuss which new stories, songs or rhymes to introduce and these should be entered into the medium-term plan.

Figure 6.2 gives an example of medium-term planning. All of the learning intentions show pooled information gathered from the sources described in Figure 6.1.

Planning for themes and topics

Sometimes advice offered on medium-term planning in early years settings suggests that the staff should pick a particular theme or

Learning intentions

Personal, Social and Emotional Development	Language and Literacy Development	Mathematical Development
Developing: ■ Developing sharing and turn taking skills *(indoor and outdoor – devise games to encourage this in outdoor play)* ■ Showing respect and sensitivity towards others	Developing: ■ listening skills, listening to each others' ideas and explanations *(turn-taking language games at group times)* ■ asking questions and responding to each other *(especially in role play)* ■ awareness of how information books work (older group) ■ familiarity with two new story books and recognition that it is the print which is read (all children) ■ confidence for all children to have a go at writing ■ understanding of purposes of writing *(provide writing materials for outdoor role play)*	Developing: ■ awareness of some properties of different shapes and describing shape *(e.g. specially in block and construction play)* ■ number – understanding counting has a purpose (to know how many) and developing counting skills (appropriate to the children's current knowledge)

Knowledge and Understanding of the World	Physical Development	Creative Development
Developing: ■ observational skills and skills in describing what has been seen ■ explanations of why things happen *(through minibeasts topic and following up other ideas with children not involved, e.g. through sand play – investigating dry and wet sand, using magnifiers)*	Developing: ■ balancing skills (younger group in particular) ■ hand-eye coordination through bat and ball activities (older group) ■ fine motor control especially in relation to clothing *(doing up buttons, putting on and doing up shoes – own clothes and dressing-up clothes)*	Developing: ■ observational skills – looking at and creating pattern, rhythm ■ representational skills: drawing, painting and modelling ■ imaginative play – getting the group of children often involved in 'superhero' play outside to develop their storylines and make some props to go with them ■ four new songs *(curriculum development: rhythm games with percussion in small groups, Deborah to lead this)*

Fig 6.2 An example of medium-term planning

topic and then plan for this. Some primary schools set up a cycle of topics to be covered by the differing sections of the school (e.g. nursery through to Year 2) on an annual or even biannual basis, and this becomes the focus of the medium-term planning for each class for a half term. This makes the choices of topic much too inflexible for an early years context and does not allow staff to follow children's interests.

Many staff do say that they find a theme or topic an easy way to plan, as it helps them to think about and link up all the areas of learning. However, a theme or topic only represents some of the learning – in particular the knowledge content about the individual topic – which will be intended. There is a tendency to concentrate on activities to do with the topic and the specific knowledge involved, rather than the learning needs of the children. The learning needs relating to underlying skills (e.g. learning to predict and make informed guesses), attitudes (e.g. developing confidence) and understandings (e.g. understanding that what you say can be written down) may be overlooked. There will also be many other learning intentions to plan for which fall outside the topic.

Themes or topics constitute, in the main, the *presentation* of learning: Julie Fisher (1998) calls themes, topics and activities *'the vehicles for learning'*. Viewed in this way, the topic or theme is there to feed an interest and to act as a starting point, rather than the entire content of the medium-term planning. The topic can be planned broadly, rather than in detail, with learning intentions rather than activities remaining the main focus of the medium-term planning. This allows much greater flexibility in following interests and needs as they become apparent, allowing staff to be more responsive by putting the detail into *short*-term planning.

Here is an example of medium-term planning developed to follow an interest in minibeasts. This topic planning was referred to in Chapter 2 in relation to one child's learning. It involved several learning intentions across several areas of learning:

Knowledge and Understanding of the World (Science and Technology)
■   to help children develop their observational skills;
■   to encourage children to discuss what they notice;
■   to set up some investigations linked to children's interests.

Literacy
- using information books to gain knowledge;
- writing for a purpose (creating own information books);
- developing familiarity with well known story books related to minibeasts.

Creative development
- to develop awareness of texture and colour;
- to develop skills in representation through drawing, painting, movement.

Mathematical development
- to develop counting skills (counting numbers of insects collected, numbers of legs, spots, etc).

Discussing this with some of the staff later clarified what a successful learning event it had been for a great many – but not all – of the children. Some were less involved, and the learning intentions for them needed to be addressed in other ways. The topic did not cover all areas of learning or all the aspects within some areas (such as maths and creative development) which the staff planned to cover in their medium-term time scale.

Short-term planning

Short-term planning is where the strongest link between assessment and planning is forged, where the in-depth knowledge of the children, stored in their records, is used to plan. The detail of how best to make the link is the focus of the next chapter, but it is the short-term planning which takes on board the *'implications for planning'* written into every example of assessment in the previous chapter. Short-term planning also links directly to the medium-term planning, and it is in the weekly planning meetings that the medium-term planning is evaluated with questions such as:

- *How far have we got?*
- *What is appropriate to do next?*
- *What do we need to adapt or change?*

The short-term planning involves all the staff working with a group or class meeting together as often as possible, preferably on a weekly basis as well as organising a very brief time on a daily basis. This is in order to evaluate what has happened over the day and to adapt as necessary anything already planned for the next day. For reception teachers who work largely on their own, they will have to do this by themselves. They should, however, find a few minutes during the day to talk with any classroom assistants about the children they have been working with and about plans for the next day. Of course, the larger the team involved in the planning meetings, the more organised the meetings need to be!

What needs to be planned?

There are distinct elements to the short-term planning in early years settings which mean that the planning for the nursery and reception classes in a school situation needs to be different to that for older age groups. This is because of the breadth of provision from which children make choices, all of which go on simultaneously, and which need thinking about and planning for. Unlike for older age groups, where it is likely that one teacher will be working alone, staff in many early years settings will need to plan for *team teaching*. They will need to plan what they will be doing, and when, to ensure that one or more staff can become involved in depth with small groups of children in a staff-led activity. Other staff can then be involved with the children in their own chosen activities and play.

The different aspects to short-term planning are:

■   an overview for the week, using the six areas of learning;
■   an optional 'daily resources' list for every day of the week (for groups which need this);
■   *'focused activity'* planning, which can be done daily or weekly.

A crucial element in both the overview for the week and the focused activity planning is planning to meet specific learning needs of specific children. This is to ensure that the *'implications for planning'*, identified when observing a child, are actually planned and carried out.

Planning the weekly overview

Some staff teams have produced a weekly planning sheet which includes a box for each area of learning (similar to that used earlier for medium-term planning) and a separate section or heading in each box for outdoor play. This ensures that every area of learning is considered within both the indoor and outdoor provision. The purpose is to focus on the learning intended for the week. Many

Weekly Planning Sheet

Week Beginning: 30.11.98

'Focus' children this week:

<u>Nadine</u>: help with cutting, encourage to join in physical play, involve in bookmaking
<u>Lauren</u>: encourage her use of books for reference and to use her skills to tell stories to others
<u>Jamie</u>: help him persevere in making models, painting, drawing – praise to build confidence
<u>Maria</u>: support her in role play – eg café outside and home corner, involve in physical games

Personal, Social, Emotional	Language and Literacy
Developing turntaking skills – taking turns to speak and listen in grouptimes – waiting for turn in game playing Developing awareness of cultures – use book of week to talk about where our families come from	Book of week: "My cat likes to hide in Boxes" by Eve Sutton Developing listening skills and awareness of rhyme – rhyming games with children's names Small group times – talking about what you have been doing during session (to develop listening and talking skills) Writing: developing awareness of purposes for writing through writing in role play
Outdoor: developing sharing and turntaking skills – set up café in role play area	**Outdoor:** Developing question and answer skills and writing for a purpose – set up café make menus, orders, bills, lots of adult involvement here
Mathematics	**K and U of World**
Number and counting skills: continue to use tidy-up time as time to count for a purpose! Make number book in relation to cats (link to book of week) Continue developing awareness of and using descriptive vocabulary about pattern – repeating patterns in block play as well as printing. Also dough cutting?	Find and share books about countries related to book of week – developing awareness of different places, differences and similarities. Continue with light and dark topic – developing skills in making electric circuits, using boxes as dark places to light-up (peepholes needed!)
Outdoor: developing awareness of space and shape and direction – make new route for wheel toy and bike play.	**Outdoor:** Developing awareness of seasons – examine rotting leaves and bare trees
Physical	**Creative**
Cutting skills: continue to support and encourage, Nadine, Jamal, Polly. Developing hand-eye coordination with throwing and catching games – encourage children who don't normally join in (Nadine, Maria) (outside)	Encourage children to paint and draw more often from own choice. Continue to provide wide variety of ways to paint each day Developing awareness of rhythm and creating own rhythm – continue percussion games – Deborah/Susie support Maria in roleplay
Outdoor: develop less confident climbers climbing skills – provide low obstacle course at beginning of week, gradually building it upwards once confident	**Outdoor:** Painting ouside? (weather...) Pattern making – chalk on ground

Focus children for next week: Polly, Hameed, Dionne Jamal

Date/time to review records:
Polly   3.12.98 am with Deborah
Hameed   1.12.98 pm with Susie
Dionne   2.12.98 am with Carolyn
Jamal   30.11.98 pm with Pearl

Fig 6.3   *A weekly planning sheet*

settings specify on this sheet *where* the learning intention is planned to take place, such as at the sand or water tray or in the home corner. Other settings use the 'daily resources list' for this purpose.

The process

The starting point to filling in the weekly overview sheet is to evaluate what happened last week, following up particular needs and interests. Some settings use a similar format for planning and evaluation, placing the 'evaluation sheet' on the reverse side of the

Evaluation of Weekly Plans	
Week Beginning: 23/1.98	
Personal and Social Turntaking in wheel toy play is getting much better – develop further through role play outside? – continue boardgame playing inside	**Language and Literacy** Small groups in book corner during session times is really encouraging children who don't usually look at books, to do so. Continue rhyming games and other ways to get children listening to each other
Mathematics Awareness of repeating patterns and talking about pattern – printing experiences went very well, lots of talk (Lucy, Terry Ahmed) Sarah + Jack repeating patterns using 2 shapes-continue Number: tidy up times are very good for counting skills -continue	**K and U of World** Main focus of the week was the weather – talking about clothes, what the wind does, collecting rain in buckets. Not what we'd planned!
Physical Cutting skills-continue Polly, Jamal, Nadine need to be encouraged to persevere with paper, card, foil.	**Creative** Encouraging children to paint more and draw more – the mix of tools and materials and the way these have been displayed has really helped. Continue to put out a mixture of ways to paint all together. Jacob, Jamal, Claire here regularly now.

Fig 6.4   A weekly evaluation sheet

planning sheet. This evaluation is to be quickly done, focusing on main developments, changes or events rather than details. What you are evaluating is the children's responses to what you provided, whether your learning intentions were met or instead whether other things came out of what was planned. The point of this is to ensure continuity for the children from one week to the next, so that what happened can be appropriately followed up. It might involve providing for the same learning intention again, in a different way for some children, or breaking down a learning intention into smaller steps. It might involve moving on to a new set of learning intentions.

The next chapter shows how effective links between assessment and planning can be made where settings focus in depth on a small group of children every week (which I will call *'focus children'*), remembering that planning for one child is often appropriate to several in the group, if not to the whole group. This ensures that the assessment information gathered is used to feed into planning for these children. The planning sheet shown in Figure 6.3 has a space to enter the names of 'focus children' for the following week. Some of the learning intentions for these children will be entered onto this sheet and some into the focused activity planning.

The next step is to look at the medium-term planning and decide what here it would be appropriate to add into the following week's plans. It is useful to add some detail of any particular language to introduce or open-ended questions to ask, designed to get the children thinking and investigating, and to think about the way in which staff will work with the children.

The resources and setting-up list

Some settings, especially those with larger staff teams, feel they need to have a *daily resources planning sheet* listing all the areas of provision which are set up by staff on a daily basis. Traditionally, many people have used this kind of planning chart as the *only* short-term planning, using it just to plan what the adults feel is right to set up, often in order to ensure variety over the week (e.g. Monday – dough, Tuesday – clay) but not necessarily planning for the learning needs of the children or following up their interests and offering further challenges.

The focus of such a chart must be:

■ *Why are we setting up these resources today?*
■ *Does it build on what happened yesterday or last week, or is it in order to introduce something new?*
■ *Is it relevant and useful to the children?*
■ *Which staff member will get involved or be responsible for it?*
■ *What will the adult who gets involved be saying or doing?*

Not all of this needs to be written down, but writing some of it down – especially what the adult might do or say – is very helpful to all staff and other adults involved.

AREA OF LEARNING	LEARNING INTENTION	ACTIVITY/RESOURCES
Knowledge and Understanding of the World	■ To develop understanding about best ways of joining materials together. ■ To talk about similarities and differences between materials.	■ Make 3D models of own choice using a chosen range of materials ■ Selection of reclaimed materials – cardboard, shiny paper, card ■ Selection of fastenings: glue – white and paste, tape, string ■ Tools: scissors, hole puncher
Creative and Language	■ Creative: to develop awareness of texture through touch and feel. ■ Language: to develop use of descriptive words to talk about texture.	■ Finger painting in flat trays, using different mixtures: poster paint; powder paint and cold water paste; powder paint, cold water paste and sand (N.B. one colour paint only). ■ Easel nearby to write up children's descriptive words.

Fig 6.5　*A focused activity planning sheet*

Focused activity planning

This involves the organisation of staff-led activities and is where the really detailed planning takes place: it should be used by all kinds of settings for three, four and five year olds. In order to ensure what is planned takes place, and that the adult concerned is not busy having to supervise other things, careful planning for the deployment of all staff is essential. In all settings, and especially in reception classes with few adults and many children, the room must be set up so that children can get on independently and access the resources for themselves.

CHILDREN	ADULT ROLE/TALK	EVALUATION
Children who have had a lot of experience in modelling, especially Hughie, Samira, Natalie, George	■ Introduce activity first; tell the children this is an investigation to see which ways of joining work best with which materials. ■ Encourage children to talk about their predictions before they try something out. Ask their views afterwards. ■ Vocabulary: joining, strong, weak.	Most children wanted to try the method of joining they were most familiar with. But getting them to slow down and think through questions staff asked got most to predict what might be best. Most knew paste wasn't any good on boxes. Hughie wound string round and round his boxes, which worked very well at first, but couldn't tie knots. Lots of conversation from Natalie (often shy if adult is involved); kept coming back to see if glue had dried.
All (or any who choose to join in)	■ Introduce activity to children before they start; tell them that every tray has slightly different mixture and you want them to think about how it feels; encourage children to talk about the differences. ■ Write up their words on easel, to use for display later. How is this one different from the one you just tried? Which one do you like best? Why?	Very successful activity: children loved their words being written on easel. Really helped only using one colour paint as it got them to concentrate on the feel of it. Lots of descriptive words, especially from Robbie, Fahad and Annie. Follow up a.s.a.p. with children who did it, making dough and talking about texture. Show them the words they used at this activity. Do this again with children who didn't have a go.

Many settings plan one focused activity per session, and try to ensure that as far as possible one adult can stay with this until it is finished. Sometimes this may be planned for any child, for a particular group of children or with one of the 'focus children' in mind. The learning intentions need to be clear, and specific details on what the adult will do and the types of questions to ask or discussions to introduce need to be included. A column for evaluation is needed, to be completed at the end of the activity. The evaluation process is then seen as an important part of the activity and some of the children can be involved in the evaluation too.

Figure 6.5 shows some examples of focused activity planning. The staff concerned found that writing up the evaluations was very useful, helping them not only to think about the children and what they were learning, but also to guide their future planning. The comments about the children were added to their records.

The daily evaluation meeting

Allowing five or ten minutes at the end of the day, when staff evaluate what has happened over the session, is invaluable. As with the evaluation in the weekly planning, this is not a time for evaluating everything but for picking out things which staff felt were significant. The focused activities should have been evaluated already, as a way of rounding these off, and these findings will need to be considered too. All of this can lead to adjusting the plans for the next day as appropriate. Some settings which use a 'resources list' fill it in daily at these meetings, to ensure that the follow-up addresses children's immediate needs and interests.

Evaluating your planning on a regular basis and adjusting and developing the plans in response to the children is an essential component of successful practice. The cycle is now complete for all three stages of planning. Some ideas for ensuring that assessment and record keeping feed into planning have been discussed briefly. Chapter 7 looks at this in more detail.

Linking Assessment to Planning

7

This chapter completes the cycle of planning, practice and assessment by linking assessment to planning. This will ensure that your medium-term and short-term plans are really appropriate to what your children need, to help them develop and progress. It means using the information you have gathered in children's records to plan for 'what next?'. This lies at the heart of good early years provision, but many staff find it hard to do in a manageable way. The only answer is to develop a *routine* for linking planning and assessment, and sticking to your routine. The chapter outlines a routine to follow.

In Chapter 6 we looked at how the short-term planning includes detailed planning for individual children, and how medium-term planning is based on more general learning needs and any special interests across the group as a whole. So, linking assessment to planning works on two levels: the specific level for short-term planning, based on your detailed knowledge of each child as noted in the child's record, and the more generalised level for medium-term planning. We will begin by looking at how the detailed knowledge of the children's learning feeds into short-term planning.

From assessment to planning: monitoring individual progress

We need to ensure that *'teaching. . . is informed by effective assessments and records'* (Ofsted, 1998). Although we may vary our 'teaching' from child to child as we interact with them, trying to ensure that what we say is comprehensible and meaningful to each individual, is not the same as using records and assessments to inform what we plan and what we do. The only way to do this is to have a system which enables the staff to review all children's records regularly, to monitor progress and development. With a large number of children's records to review, how can this be done so that it can be used to inform teaching?

In Chapter 6 it was noted how some nursery settings focus on a small number of children each week in order to make plans which are specific to them. This does not mean excluding the more general planning for the others, as this is incorporated into the overall weekly plans. But there must also be a systematic routine developed to review the records, going through each child's record in rotation. Without such a system, some children can easily get missed out – and it is often the quieter children who do not seek out adult attention, who are overlooked.

Time needs to be allocated each week, during the normal session time or school day, to review a small number of children's records with the children concerned. The member of staff draws out from the evidence in the record what the child needs to support further development. This can then be discussed at the next weekly planning meeting, and plans made for these children as part of the short-term planning for the week. Staff decide which children's records to review during the following week. The plans are then implemented over the week. Let us look at this in more detail.

Reviewing records with the children

Every week arrange a time to review a small number of records, chosen from the whole group in rotation. This is a time for a member of staff to be reviewing the record in the room *with the child*. It should take 5–10 minutes per child.

This process has two purposes. First, it gives you the *time to review* the record and summarise what you know about the child, and to identify any gaps in the record for any areas of learning. For example, if there is very little recorded for mathematical development, you will need to find out more, either by setting up an activity for the child or by observing the child in play. Second, it *involves the child*, giving the child time to reflect on his or her own development and learning. Children are usually thrilled to see what has been collected about them. They immediately start to tell you more about things which have happened, how they managed to do something, and what they can do now. They often want to show what they can do now which they couldn't do then. This is *such* an important time for the child.

If all the evidence of learning collected in the records has been analysed using a similar format to the one given in Chapter 5, then the *'implications for planning'* will already be there in the record. It is best to do this at the time when the assessment is made, when you are most involved. If it has not been done already, then time will have to be found to do this while the record is reviewed with the child, making the review time a little longer. Whether completed before or not, these planning ideas should be shared with the child, who may well have their own views too. Potentially, there will be a collection of quite different implications for planning for each area of learning. This is the time to prioritise them.

It will be important to review each child's record in this way *at least* once per term, but many prefer to do it once per half term. Every setting is different, with different numbers of children and staff. In a reception class or nursery class where the teacher is the sole person responsible for the records, it might be possible to plan a 'quiet reading' time when the children are looking at books. This may provide the opportunity for the teacher to look through a child's record with the child, talking to them about what is in the record, and showing them their samples collected over time. Having a form of the type shown in Figure 7.1 on which to transfer the planning priorities is very helpful. It might be possible to look through one record with a child per day or, if children in nursery are part-time, one per session.

In a playgroup it may be enough to review two or three records per week. In a nursery setting, with a large staff team who are responsible for the records, it will be important to allocate the time so each member of staff is reviewing the record for one child from their group a week. This would mean that for six staff, six review times will need to be allocated each week.

REVIEW OF RECORD

Child's name: Date:

Any significant developments since last summary:

What next?
Planning experiences, activities, staff involvement and any further observations needed for record

---

Fig 7.1   A review record format

Fig 7.2   *A member of staff reviewing the record with a child*

Some early years centres and nursery schools allow time in weekly meetings for discussions between staff about children in their class groups. This is a meeting *about* children, separate from the planning meeting. However, it must not be used to replace the valuable time to go through the record with the child concerned. Doing this with the child is a crucial part of your teaching, not an additional luxury. The effect on the child in terms of developing self-esteem and self-awareness is vital.

This kind of review enables you to prioritise *'what next?'* for this child. Obviously you want the children to grow from where they are now in every respect, and much of this development will come from your general provision for learning for all children. Some will, of course, come with the developing maturity of the child. However, your specific planning is to prioritise what the child needs *most* support for, and this could be in any area of learning. What you are planning is a learning opportunity you will be *offering* to the child concerned. It is not a matter of coercing the child or assuming that, because the child became involved in what you planned, he or she has necessarily made a leap in development.

Planning from the assessments

Planning for an individual child, based on your review of the record may mean:

- planning a focused activity for this child and several others;
- planning to encourage the child to join in an activity or area of provision they have not tried before;
- planning to develop an area of strength, by setting up new challenges and investigations;
- planning opportunities for further play and exploration, and planning for a member of staff to be involved in this;
- planning opportunities for the child to continue, repeat and practise with the necessary adult support.

Most learning will require much longer than a week to be established in the child, but planning it into the weekly plan means you are focusing on the child's needs in greater depth. What you plan will only rarely be exclusive to the one child, for, usually, many children will be involved in an activity in different ways, appropriate to their own needs. Often, planning for one child in this way is about *fine-tuning* the overall provision you are making.

At the weekly planning meeting, make the plans specific to those individual children, as noted from your reviews. The weekly planning 'overview' format illustrated in Chapter 6 (Figure 6.3) gives a space at the top to name the children whose records have been reviewed and who will be the focus of some of the planning for the week. Their learning needs can be entered here too. At the bottom, there is another box for the names of children with whom staff will review records in the following week.

If you plan too many learning intentions over the week for one child, they will not all happen. The planning needs to be realistic and manageable for you and the child. For example, there could be three learning intentions, one to be met through a focused activity, one for a member of staff to become more involved in the child's self-chosen activities and play, and a third to do more observing, watching out for what is happening in relation to a particular area of learning. The third will be easily met by the first and second, because you have made time to be with the child.

The planning for Jemma (Figure 7.3) resulted in a member of staff setting up another snail investigation with her and one other child, who also needed help in developing relationships with others. The 'care of living things' was reinforced through discussion, and the other child gave Jemma support in doing this too. Drawing was encouraged, not only during this event but for the rest of the week, resulting in samples being added to the record. There was also a 'knock on' effect on Jemma, giving her confidence to choose to draw independently more often.

REVIEW OF RECORD

Child's name: Jemma   (3 years 10 months)   **Date:** 24/5/99

Any significant developments since last summary:
The snail project has really taken off with Jemma:
- focused her attention and extended concentration dramatically
- developing talk for wider range of purposes – describing what she sees, predicting, especially when with member of staff

What next?
- Encourage to draw, paint more frequently and add samples to record
- Set up a snail investigation with one other child to:
  – help her to develop her relationships with others, especially *listening* to other children
  – take greater care with living things and be more gentle, encourage closer observation

---

Fig 7.3   A completed review record sheet

Implementing the plans

During the week, staff will be working from their plans, implementing what has been decided. Putting into action the plans for the specific group of children will no doubt prove an ideal opportunity to add to their record. You will be noticing things you had not seen before, because you are spending more time with these children. You may also find that significant developments are taking place. Seeing how children take up what was planned is the most rewarding aspect of planning. At the same time, your normal record-keeping and assessment process is continuing for all the children. None of this requires extra time at the end of the day. It is all part of the daily work with children.

The cycle continues

At the planning meeting, decide which children are to be reviewed next week. Their names should be entered on the planning sheet to ensure their review times happen. Having devised a system which works for you, it has to be maintained and developed into a routine exercise. If a child is away on their 'review' day, choose another child to review instead. If the child is not there during the week when activities were planned for her or him, then note in your weekly evaluation that the plan will need to be put into action on their return.

Once the system is up and running, it becomes a good habit. It helps planning become more focused – and often more inventive and interesting – because you are working in a more focused way with the children.

From assessing to planning: feeding into medium-term planning

Knowing the children

The learning intentions to plan for in the medium term will come as the staff get to know the children and work with them – listening, observing, teaching, talking with them, and, especially, reviewing their records with them. Meeting with parents on a regular basis enables staff to find out more about what the child does at home. This evidence is added to the staff's own understanding of the child.

Deciding which are the appropriate learning intentions for medium-term planning comes from summarising this knowledge about the children. It does not take long to build up a picture of what will be appropriate to plan for a group of children, nor to know what interests or motivates them most.

Reviewing records on a regular basis with the children through a systematic process as described in this chapter ensures that planning and practice are tailored to the developmental needs of the children. It also ensures they meet the 'official' requirements quoted at the beginning of this chapter and in Chapter 1. But most importantly, this is what brings the rewards and makes all your work with the children both rewarding and effective.

Maintaining Success 8

We have come full circle. In this book we have examined the elements which make up this circle: planning, practice, assessment and evaluation. Maintaining success means keeping the cycle going, keeping the children at the centre, listening and observing, being responsive, and having fun together.

Let us conclude by showing how the cycle was put into action for one child in a nursery setting. The example is a summary of part of this child's record, compiled over five terms. The staff collected their evidence on learning and development in the ways described in Chapters 4 and 5, and used the information to plan in a similar way to that outlined in Chapters 6 and 7. Through this way of working, the staff planned for Kieran, and all the other children, to help their progress and development.

Kieran   *Started nursery at 3 years 4 months*

Aspects of Literacy and Creative Development

Feb 98 (age 3.4) At graphics area, enjoying writing and drawing. Writes his name in letter-like shapes, using both hands.

April 98 (3.6) Drew an owl, using both hands.

July 98 (3.9) Talked about what his writing said.

Sept 98 (3.11) Writes his name with help of his name card; said 'It's my name'.

Dec 98 (4.2) Retelling familiar stories accurately.

Jan 99 (4.3) Involved in making a book with a group of children, wrote and drew in the book. Found his own name label and copied it easily.

March 99 (4.5) Drew a picture of a character from a book (a bear).

Talked about it to staff, then decided to copy some of the letters from words on the page.

April 99 (4.6) Making a class book from a familiar story, drew a dragon. Confident and skilled in representational drawing, less sure about own writing, but soon persuaded to have a go (see Figure 8.1). For 'dragon', member of staff wrote word first and he copied.

May 99 (4.7) Dictated familiar story for staff member to scribe onto computer. Able to join in retelling of another story, acting the part of one of the characters. Really enjoyed this.

Aspects of Personal, Social and Emotional, Language development and Knowledge and Understanding of the World

March 98 (3.5) Talks about what he is playing with, asks questions of other children and adults in shortened form 'What you doing?'

June 98 (3.8) Beginning to get involved for longer periods in play with others, e.g. in sand play, sustained conversation with another child about the play.

July 98 (3.9) Related story about a past event in some detail to a member of staff. Also talked about the shapes he was making with plasticine and what they looked like. Used talk to tell others what he was doing in the play which followed: 'I'm putting it in the oven now. It's got hot.'

October 98 (4.0) Observation of K making models with construction kit showed how he negotiated with others and described what he was making to them.

November 98 (4.1) Whilst looking at a book with other children and adult, he described what his home looked like and what his bed and bedroom are like.

Feb 99 (4.4) Using descriptive language in play with cornflour: 'It's slimy, it's sticky. It's dropping down. I can make round and round patterns.'

Kieran has been interested in minibeasts since March. In their medium-term planning the staff planned a topic on minibeasts as a way of following up an interest of several children.

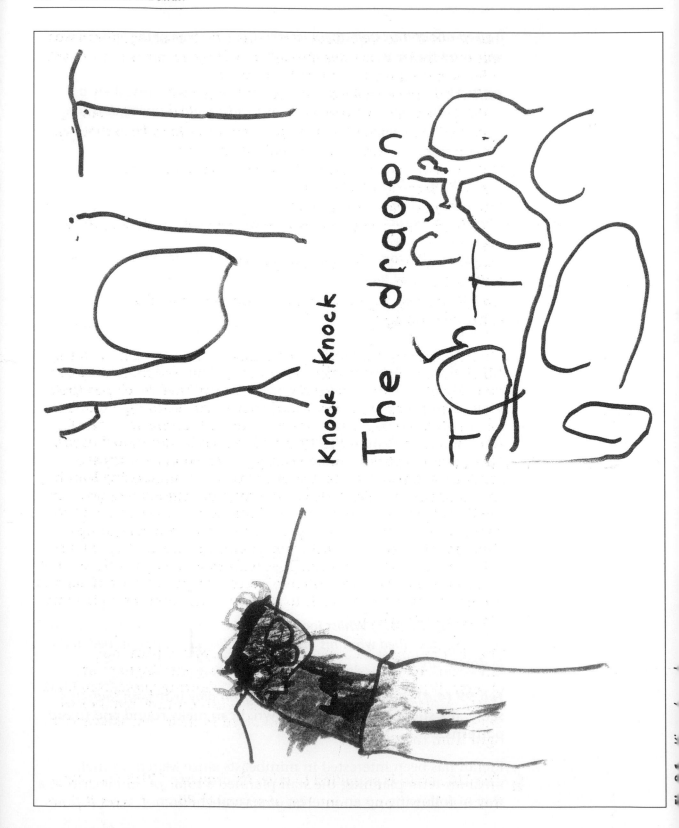

Knock Knock

The dragon

June 99 (4.8) Making a book about snails for the nursery, Kieran was able to share his knowledge through answering questions and to think of his own questions he wanted to investigate.

Staff: How did we make the home for the snails?

K: We got a tank for them. We put in soil and stones. We put in stones so they could hide. We splashed water in to keep them wet. We put in blocks and stones to help them climb.

Staff: How can we get the snail to come out of its shell?

K: A leaf, because it will eat it.

Staff: Why do they have shells?

K: To hide. Their shells feel hard. You know where they've gone *(referring to trail).*

Another child: Why do they have slime?

K: To help them move.

Staff: What else do you want to find out about snails?

K: Do they eat eggs?

Kieran's learning and development have been catered for in a way which follows up what motivates him and his zest for finding out more about the world around him. The staff have developed their **long-term planning overview** of appropriate learning intentions for the children in the age group, ensuring that this will cater for *all* children, including those who have special educational needs. They ensure that the children can be involved in their chosen activities and play by creating an exciting and stimulating learning environment in which to learn and have fun simultaneously. The **medium-term planning** links the long term to the short term by choosing appropriate learning intentions for the whole group of children. The detailed **short-term planning** ensures that staff are able to focus in depth on activities with small groups of children. A system for reviewing the children's records regularly with them and using these reviews to feed into medium- and short-term planning has been established.

The children must be at the heart of this cycle of planning, assessment and practice. The adults working with them must observe, listen and talk with them. The following quote from Mark Twain, writing at the end of the nineteenth century, reminds us that children have a right to be involved in their own assessment, right from the start:

❝ *The little child is permitted to label its drawing: "This is a cow – this is a horse" and so on. This protects the child. It saves it from the sorrow and wrong of hearing its cows and its horses criticised as kangaroos and work benches.* 9

Assessment and planning should not be processes which are *done* to the child.

Let us make sure that in the planning and assessment processes we set up to enable children to progress and develop, their voices come through loud and clear. Let us leave the last word to a child.

Sauda (4 years and 8 months) is talking about her time in the nursery, her favourite activities and her own development:

Fig 8.2
Sauda's shapes

‘ *I like drawing best, drawing lots of things. At nursery I learn songs. Before I came to nursery I couldn't do hard puzzles. Babies can't do hard puzzles and they can't make hats like I can. And they can't draw triangles like I can. Here's a triangle, a square – oh no, it's a rectangle – here's a . . .sort of square and a circle. See?' She then walks off to find her friends.* ’

References

Assessment in the early years

Bartholomew, L. and Bruce, T., *Getting to Know You,* Hodder and Stoughton, 1996.

Drummond, M. J., Rouse, D., and Pugh, G., *Making Assessment Work,* NES Arnold/National Children's Bureau, 1992.

Drummond, M. J., *Assessing Children's Learning,* David Fulton, 1993.

Hutchin, V., *Tracking Significant Achievement in The Early Years,* Hodder and Stoughton, 1996.

Lally, M. and Hurst, V. 'Assessment and the Nursery Curriculum' , in Blenkin, G. M. and Kelly, A. V. (eds), *Assessment in Early Childhood Education,* Paul Chapman Publishing, 1992.

Books on child development and early learning

Bryant, P. and Bradley, L., *Children's Reading Problems,* Blackwell, 1985.

Donaldson, M., *Children's Minds,* Collins/Fontana, 1978.

Navarra, J. G., *The Development of Scientific Concepts in a Young Child: a case study,* Teacher College, Columbia University, New York, 1955.

Nutbrown, C., *Threads of Thinking,* Paul Chapman Publishing, 1994.

Vygotsky, L., *Thought and Language ,* MIT Press, 1978.

Wells, G., *The Meaning Makers: Children Learning language and Using Language to Learn,* Hodder and Stoughton, 1986.

Education in the early years

Drummond, M. J., Lally, M., and Pugh, G., *Working with Children: Developing a Curriculum for the Early Years,* NES Arnold/National Children's Bureau, 1989.

Edgington, M., *The Nursery Teacher In Action,* Paul Chapman Publishing, 1998.

Fisher, J., *Starting with the Child,* Open University Press, 1998.

Gura, P., *Resources for Early Learning: Children, Adults and Stuff,* Hodder and Stoughton, 1996.

Jowett, S. and Sylva, K., 'Does Kind of Preschool Matter?',
    Educational Research, *28*, 1, 21–31, 1986
Pugh, G., Annual TES/Guardian Lecture, 1997.

'Official' publications

ACCAC, *Desirable Outcomes for Children's Learning on Entering
    Compulsory School (Wales)*, Wales, 1996.
DES, *Starting with Quality*, Report of the Rumbold Committee of
    Inquiry, 1990.
HM Inspectors of Schools, *A Curriculum Framework for children in
    their Pre-School Year*, Scottish Office, 1997.
Northern Ireland Council for the Curriculum, Examinations and
    Assessment, *Curriculum Guidance for Pre-School Education*, 1997.
Ofsted, *Are You Ready for Your Inspection?*, 1998.
QCA, *An Introduction to Curriculum Planning for Under-Fives*, 1998.
QCA, *Assessment and Reporting Arrangements Key Stage 1*, 1998.
QCA, *Teacher Assessment at Key Stage 2*, 1998.
QCA, *Curriculum Guidance for the Foundation Stage*, 2000.
SCAA, *Desirable Outcomes for Children's Learning on Entering
    Compulsory Education*, 1996.
SCAA, *Looking at Children's Learning*, 1997.

Assessment 'schemes' referred to in the text

Core Basics, *Core Basics Assessment Record Book 3*, 1997.
London Borough of Islington, *Under-Fives Record*, 1998.
London Borough of Westminster, *Great Expectations*, 1994.
Royal Borough of Kensington and Chelsea, *Early Years Profile*, 1992.
Sound Learning, *Pre-School Record System*, 1997.

Children's books referred to in the text

Browne, E., *Handa's Surprise*, Walker Books, 1995.
Carle, E., *The Very Hungry Caterpillar*, Puffin, 1974.
Sutton, E., *My Cat Likes to Hide in Boxes*, Puffin, 1978.